The WYCKOFF METHOD *Collection*

The WYCKOFF METHOD *Collection*

• How I Trade and Invest in Stocks and Bonds

• Studies In Tape Reading •

ISBN: 978-1-6673-0641-4 paperback
ISBN: 978-1-6673-0642-1 hardcover

TABLE OF CONTENTS

RICHARD D. WYCKOFF

"We succeed in proportion to the amount of energy and enterprise we use in going after results"

How I TRADE AND INVEST IN STOCKS AND BONDS

Being Some Methods Evolved and Adopted

During My Thirty-three Years

Experience in Wall Street

By

RICHARD D. WYCKOFF

Editor, *The Magazine of Wall Street*

ILLUSTRATED

NEW YORK
THE MAGAZINE OF WALL STREET
1925

TO MY WIFE

Whose unfailing courage,
co-operation
and belief in me has
enabled me to
attain some of my ideals

Fifth Edition

CONTENTS

FOREWORD

During the last thirty-three years I have been a persistent student of the security markets. As a member of several Stock Exchange firms, as a bond dealer, trader and investor, I have come into active contact with many thousands of those who are executing orders and handling markets, as well as those who deal in such markets, namely traders and investors.

For the past fifteen years I have edited and published *The Magazine of Wall Street*, which at this writing has the largest circulation of any financial publication in the world.

These experiences have given me an opportunity to study not only the stock and bond markets, but all those related thereto, and have enabled me to observe the forces which influence these markets and the human elements which contribute so largely to their activity and wide fluctuations.

Out of this experience I have evolved or adopted or formulated certain methods of trading and investing, and some of these I have collected and presented in the pages which follow.

My purpose in preparing this book has been two-fold. Primarily, I have in mind the thousands of new investors who find the securities market a vast, technical machine, too complex to be understood by many. It has been my effort to do away with this impression — to emphasize the fact that, in Wall Street as anywhere else, the chief essential is common sense, coupled with study and practical experience. I have attempted to outline the requirements for success in this field in a way that will be understandable to all.

Furthermore, as I learned in preparing my first book, "Studies in Tape Beading," it is of great personal advantage for me to write out and thus clarify and crystallize in my own mind the principles upon which I endeavor to operate. And so, from both standpoints it seemed to me well worth while to arrange my impressions in methodical and coherent order.

RICHARD D. WYCKOFF

Great Neck, L. I.
March, 1922.

I hold that a man who is longheaded, who foresees and judges accurately, has an advantage over his neighbor and it is not accounted immoral for him to use that advantage because he is individually better fitted for the business; and it inheres in him by a law of nature, that he has a right to the whole of himself legitimately applied. If one man, or twenty men, looking at the state of the nation here, at the crops, at the possible contingencies and risks of climate, at the conditions of Europe; in other words, taking all the elements that belong to the world into consideration, be sagacious enough to prophesy the best course of action, I don't see why it is not legitimate.

Henry Ward Beecher.

How I TRADE AND INVEST IN STOCKS AND BONDS

I. FIRST LESSONS

AT the suggestion of my first employer in Wall Street, I began the study of railroad and other corporation statistics about the time my trousers were being lengthened from knee to ankle and I was receiving the munificent sum of $20 per month. This was in 1888.

With numerous interruptions my studies continued until 1897, when I began to put them into practice by purchasing one share of St. Louis & San Francisco common at $4 per share. At that time some of the other leading stocks were selling at the following prices: Union Pacific 4-, Southern Pacific 14, Norfolk & Western 9, Atchison 9, Northern Pacific 11. Reading 17. To put it mildly, prices were very low. Many roads were just emerging from, or were still in, receivership, and Irish dividends were the rule.

As I saved a little money I began to buy more one share lots and finally I became such a pest in this respect that the Stock Exchange firm which I "favored'* with my orders said they didn't care for the business, whereupon I decided to buy more shares, of fewer varieties.

This is the way most people begin their operations—by purchasing outright, believing that they are safe. It is true they are safe in the possession of their certificates once they have them in their safe deposit boxes, but in no other respect. They are not safe against fluctuations or shrinkages in value or earning power. Nevertheless, if their securities are well selected, and bought at the right time, the chances are strongly in favor of their making money.

It was my practice about that time to sit up nights, read the financial papers, and study probably future values of securities, and when I didn't have money enough to buy, I would make my selections just the same and write my imaginary purchases in a book with reasons alongside why they should ultimately be worth more money. Two of these I still retain in my memory, viz., Chicago, Burlington & Quincy at 57, and Edison Electric Illuminating of New York, at 101.

I mention these incidents because they illustrate a very good way for anyone to begin to learn the business of trading and investing in securities. Just as in any other line it is practice that makes perfect, and most of the fatalities in Wall Street can be traced to lack of practice. You don't have to risk real money when you are learning, and I always advocate two or three *years*—not two or three months, mind you—of this kind of study and paper practice when one is seriously considering participation in this greatest of all games. But study and practice are the two things farthest removed from the minds of the majority. Everyone knows that people who engage in speculation for the first time do not want to bother with such details. The average man who comes to Wall Street comes to speculate, although he may pay in full for his purchases. All he asks is to be told "someithing good." That is not speculation, it is gambling; for speculation, to quote Thomas F. Woodlock, "involves the use of intelligent foresight." Most people use neither foresight nor intelligence.

It might seem to the reader a long while to wait, hut in my case I did not begin to invest until eight years after I started to study, and I did not commence trading for six years after that, so it may be admitted that I went to school and got a foundation knowledge which has been of inestimable value.

In connection with my one share purchases I found that although I had correctly figured financial conditions and earning power of the companies whose securities I held, their prices would often fluctuate widely as a result of general market conditions. In other words, a stock might go down, although everything in the way of intrinsic value and future possibilities pointed upward; so I made up my mind that there were other factors to be considered and found that these were principally three, viz., manipulation, technical conditions and trend of the market.

In order to study the market closely I identified myself with a leading New York Stock Exchange house which did a big business for some prominent operators, and there I learned how necessary it is to observe the proposition, not from the standpoint of the outsider who is endeavoring to anticipate the fluctuations from what he sees on the surface, but from the standpoint of the insider who is a factor in influencing prices.

Investigation proved that many of those who were thus able to affect prices often made the same mistakes as small traders, only their errors ran into big money, which, however, was not out of the proportion to their profits. Years before, in my clerical capacity in the brokerage business, I had noticed tendencies among small traders which I now found magnified many diameters in the case of large operators.

In the study of technical conditions, which was my next step, I found that the most important factor was the trend of the market and that the overbought or oversold condition of the market had the most to do with the immediate direction of the next swing.

No doubt the principles which will be found in my book, *"Studies in Tape Reading,"* were rattling around in my head for a long time before I wrote them out, and as I did this they clarified and crystallized. When I realized this, I began to put them into practice by trading in ten share lots, although I had operated in a much larger way some years before. It seemed to me that, with the right principles and a sufficient amount of practice, I could gradually build up my trading on a strong foundation that would not lead to flash-in-the-pan results but to a steady increase in speculative ability and consequent profits.

Being in the brokerage business, my immediate object was to make more money for my clients, because I realized that this was the only way in which they would become permanent and successful clients. My ultimate object, however, was to get out of the brokerage business and devote my time to the security markets, and it is a satisfaction to say that I arrived at that point some years ago.

Unlike many who operate in order that they may make money with which to enlarge their market operations, I am more interested in realizing profits so that I may have more money to invest. Just as its staff writers, through the columns of *The Magazine of Wall Street*, advocate that the business man take his surplus and invest it in sound securities, so I make a business of trading and invest the profits which result. In a word, I trade so that I may invest.

But let us go back a little and note some of the points which came to me while I was studying the subject in an objective way:

The market operations which were carried on in the office of my first employers were not significant because it was a small firm and did not have many customers. The head of the firm traded a little and made some money, because he seemed to understand what he was doing. Most of the customers, on the other hand, neither understood nor made money. Once in a while some one would come in and plunge around, pay a lot of commissions, and then go away disgusted with the business. Traders of this sort should have been disgusted with themselves. The majority seemed to look upon it as a sport or an adventure in which they hoped to prove that their judgment and ability were better than those of all who they knew had failed.

Nearly everyone seemed to be just guessing.

One man certainly carried off the palm at the business of buying at the top and selling at the bottom. Another told me how he had taken one little Reading 3rd Income Bond, worth about $300, and by pyramiding on the rise in Reading during former years had run up an equity of something 'over '$250,000. But at this particular time he was down to a shoestring again.

We had one old fellow who bought nothing but the very highest grade railroad bonds, and only when they were very low. Collecting these and clipping coupons was a mania with him and in order to indulge his mania he economized to the point of using a piece of plain manila twine to hold his eye glasses. He and other out-and-out investors were the most satisfactory clients because they kept coming around year after year, while those who speculated disappeared one after the other. As for the latter, I noticed a very marked tendency to accept a small profit and stand for a big loss. About that time I heard of a prominent Brooklyn man who after several attempts at speculation said to himself, "I know the secret of this game—these traders are all taking small profits and big losses. I will open a bucket shop and when they do this they will force me to take small losses and big profits." He did. And in a short while he bought a couple of hotels and was rated as a millionaire. No doubt he mistrusted his own ability to trade as the others were doing and followed strictly this profitable principle (the bucket shop proprietor may have two different kinds of principles although they are spelled the same way), but he knew if he got into the business he would be obliged by the very ignorance of his clients, to make more money than he lost.

Turning again to my brokerage office, I must say that impressions derived there were not conducive to speculation, but showed the marked advantages of shrewd investing.

The next firm with which I became identified was one which had private wires, branch offices and a considerable number of clients, large and small. Some of them were big traders and a few were very successful. Here I really began to learn something from observation of their methods. The one who impressed me most strongly was a high official of the telegraph company from which we leased some of our wires. He stuck out from the rest because of his fixed policy of cutting his losses short (here was that same principle bobbing up again). He never gave an order unless it was accompanied by a two-point stop. He dealt in the most active and widely fluctuating issues on both sides of the market. Unlike many of the customers who were "fluent losers" he was the only man whom I remember as being persistently successful. He would usually trade in two-hundred share lots at a time and generally managed to get a little larger profit than the two points and commission which he risked.

While I was with that firm the panic of 1893 occurred. General Electric declined from 114 to 20, and American Cordage crashed down from 140 to reorganization levels. This experience showed me what risks people ran who made speculative commitments without limiting their possible losses or watching them closely and getting out when they found they were wrong. The market for these and other stocks simply melted away, there being few buyers and many compulsory sellers. I had seen these things before in the Baring panic of 1890 but they did not make the same impression on me because I had not come into such close contact with those who were making speculative commitments of considerable size.

A few years later I secured a position with a large, ambitious and growing New York Stock Exchange house which had private wires, branch offices and correspondents all over the country. Its long list of customers and its important connections made it develop rapidly into one of the biggest houses in the Street. Here I was able to obtain a still broader view of the markets, for the concern did a big cotton and grain, as well as stock and bond, business. Many of their people made considerable money. A few made spectacular profits in la short while, but I observed that their sudden wealth led to over-extension and big losses because they evidently did not have the same judgment where larger amounts were involved. This was another point in favor of the slowly building up process.

The big wire houses in Boston, Philadelphia and Chicago poured their business over our wires, but not knowing the operations of their individual customers, I could only judge by the composite that was presented to me through having everything come in the name of the house. Two kinds of operations were evidently going on. One was a large inflow of buying and selling orders, evidently arising from those who were endeavoring to anticipate the immediate fluctuations. The result of these was indicated in a corresponding inflow of money to margin such transactions and take care of the losses which resulted in the net, proving that the traders in other cities were no different from those I had met here; that is, that they were more or loss impracticed and inefficient at the business.

The other kind of dealings impressed me the most. They consisted of a steady line of orders to purchase securities like Atchison

General Mortgage 4s, and Incomes, Norfolk & Western preferred. Union Pacific preferred, and the better grade of stocks and bonds in companies just emerging from receivership. These were bought in very large quantities and shipped away, principally to the West. Evidently there were some people in that great railroad center, Chicago, and in its tributaries, who were familiar with the railroad business, and who saw possibilities in the future for such stocks and bonds in spite of a disastrous past.

In the hull market which begem with McKinley's first election in 1896, and ran for several years, these Union Pacifies, Readings, Aichisons and others which had been through receivership, reorganization and assessment, multiplied many times in value and furnished the most striking lesson I had received so far.

It was plain that the most successful class of our clients was the far"-sighted investors who held, or were often able to pick up, stocks like Beading and others at less than the amount of the cash assessment that had been paid in. For these assessments they were usually given preferred stocks, and when the market prices of the latter eventually rose to around par, they had their assessment money back and either a recovery of their former losses or a big profit on the common stocks which they had acquired at the low figures.

I had a good many lessons in speculation during my four years with that firm. It being a bull period there were numerous instances of the development of small accounts into big ones. Governor Flower was the bull leader at the time and some of his stocks went from small to big figures. He had a large following, was perfectly honest with it and made a great deal of money for the public until the day he ate too many radishes at his fishing club in Riverhead, Long Island, and passed away. Next morning most of those who had made money on the bull side and had loaded up with many times what they started with lost the bulk of it at the opening.

One of my fellow clerks gave an illustration of what could be done with a little money. Starting with a small quantity of stock he pyramided until he realized the sum of $3,000, which looked very large to a thirty-dollar-a-week clerk. I found that he was not basing his judgment on the news, but on a study of the fluctuations. His spedialties were American Sugar and Brooklyn Rapid Transit. Out of his profits he bought a home for himself, paying his three thousand dollars down, ' * so they couldn't get it away from him." He kept charts of the market and studied them intelligently, just as many other people then known as "chart fiends," were doing.

To keep charts in those days was looked upon as making one fit for the squirrels. In and out of many brokerage offices there hustled wild-eyed individuals with charts under their arms, who would hold forth at length on double tops and bottoms and show you just where and how and why the "big fellows" were doing this or that with their favorite stocks. Yet none of them seemed to have much money. Possibly it was because they followed a strict set of rules and did not use much intelligence. It seems that the charts told them exactly what to do!

Successful students of the market were few but there were some; and I began to get a line on their methods of reasoning. I was surprised to find that the market itself did give frequent evidence of its future course and began to investigate along those lines. It did not interfere with my study of intrinsic value and earning power but rather supplemented it, for I often found that statistics and the action of the market would all point in the same direction.

So far as manipulation was concerned, it appeared to have one of three objects: Making the public buy, sell or keep out. And I judged that the manipulators were endeavoring to do the opposite. The market at that time consisted of a comparatively few stocks, although they were increasing. The dominant trading factor was James R. Keene. The Rockefeller party was active in some of its stocks. Morgan had not yet "sprung" the Steel Trust, Gates and Harriman were just coming over the horizon, and the Gould sun was about setting. It was a market which could be easily stung by a group of new powerful interests working in harmony, but while public participation and volume of trading was large, it was not to be compared with the markets of today in the number of participants or the large number of stocks dealt in.

Having secured a new angle on the market I began myself to try to judge it from its own action, principally with regard to the general trend. Dow's theory of price movement made a considerable impression on me. I understood clearly his theory that there were three distinct market movements going on simultaneously—(1) the long trend extending over a period of years; (2) the thirty to sixty day swings; (3) the small swings running from one to several days. The value of these suggestions appeared to be great when properly applied.

I thirsted for stock market and investment knowledge but much to my regret there were very few people who could assist me and very little printed matter which was of any value whatever. So I had to dig it out for myself, the best I could. It was a slow process or else I was not bright enough to absorb it quickly, but I made progress, as I will show in succeeding chapters.

MAKERS OF U.S. STEEL HISTORY

Four of the chief figures in the organization and administration of U. S. Steel Corporation whose shares have long been among the most popular investment mediums.

II.
PROFITABLE EXPERIENCES

HAVING accumulated enough money to go into business for myself, I resigned from the big wire house and began to deal in unlisted securities. Later on, with some associates, I formed a New York Stock Exchange firm, became the managing partner and for a number of years continued in the stock brokerage business. This put me in intimate touch with the operations of customers, and a number of other large operators.

I had not watched these traders for long before I reached three definite conclusions as to trading methods. They were as follows:

(1) The majority of those who were buying and selling securities were almost totally ignorant of the business.

(2) They were mentally lazy. They showed no desire to increase their knowledge of the subject, but anybody who gave them tips or so-called "information" held the greatest attraction for them.

(3) Very little educational literature was obtainable, even if the trading element had been inclined to devote thought and study to self preparation.

It was astounding to see how men, shrewd, careful and successful in their own business, would come down to the Street and throw caution to the winds when they undertook to deal in stocks or bonds.

I had reached a point where I was a fair judge of the market; and I did my level best to aid them. As time went on, I did manage to help many people make considerable money; but I found that most of them wanted to lean—not to learn. They just drifted along, guided by hope of profit and pursued by fear of loss.

The clientele with which I came into contact during those years gave me a clear idea of the psychology of the average trader and investor, and I found that as a rule his viewpoint of the market was very much warped; that he did, most of the time, the opposite of what the large and experienced operator would do, because he judged by the surface conditions of the market and not by the highly important technical conditions. A clear understanding of these technical conditions, I saw, was most vital to anyone who expected to operate successfully. And so it came about that for a considerable time I devoted most of my thought and attention to the investment side of securities rather than the speculative.

After founding, during the panic of 1907, *The Magazine of Wall Street, then known as The Ticker*, I began to receive numerous inquiries from people who were anxious to learn more about the swings of the market, and I also received contributions of articles from those who had studied these subjects. Another kind of communication contained a description of methods more or less mechanical on which the (Writers desired opinions. At that time there was a wide interest in the search for a method of operating which would do away with fallible human judgment. And while this seemed to be a species of rainbow-chasing, there is no doubt that I was able to learn much from a study of the different kinds of recorded market actions. Some of the points which I had acquired through the examination of numerous ideas submitted and some other points which I studied out for myself greatly aided me in judging the market.

The reason for this is that all graphs, charts, diagrams, etc., which form pictures of the movements of individual stocks or groups of securities, are but the concrete history of the impression of many minds upon the market. And my object in studying along this line was not to follow these indications blindly, but to see what kind of mental operations caused them. By thus reasoning out the good and bad points in the psychology of the public I hoped to get at the true method of operating.

So right here I would like to say a good word for all forms of graphs which are apt to be greatly abused and misused by people who have never taken the trouble to investigate their value. There is scarcely a business or profession today that does not employ graphs as indicators of conditions, operations, etc., in thousands of different forms. What, therefore, could be more logical than to adopt graphs as a means of seeing and clarifying such a complex proposition as the security market?

As time went on, my publication office became the center of interest to a great number of people who had tackled this problem from various angles, and in the examination of their ideas and by the adoption of good and the elimination of the bad points, I gradually formed a fairly clear idea as to how a permanent success might be established by one willing to devote his time and attention to the matter, making all else secondary. As demand arose from many quarters for information on the subject of judging the market from its own action, I decided to make a specialty of this subject, study it out and write about it as I went along. The outcome of this was the book, *"Studies in Tape Reading,"* which has since been reprinted in many editions. And the principles therein stated have not changed through all the vicissitudes of the market during the dozen years which have elapsed since the book first appeared in serial form in *The Magazine of Wall Street.*

Many people will say it is one thing to write about a difficult proposition like the security market, and quite another to put your ideas into practical operation, that is, to make money out of them. Suffice it to say that, since I wrote that book, I have made a very considerable amount of money for myself and in the aggregate millions of dollars for my subscribers by applying the methods therein set forth, viz., judging from the future course of the market and of individual securities by their own action. And I expect to keep on making, each year, much more money than I spend, because the principles in that book are absolutely sound and practicable, as proven by the dollars derived from the market thereby.

In *"Studies in Tape Reading"* I suggested trading for daily profits with the object of making a fractional profit over losses, expenses, commissions, etc., on the average, per day. But eventually I found that I could get much better results by operating for the five, ten and twenty point swings. Furthermore, I learned that to operate in the latter way was to lessen the nervous strain occasioned by watching the tape every minute of the day and carrying all the quotations of the leading active stocks and their previous action in my head.

I found that the real money was to be made in the important swings running thirty to sixty days on the average, in which accumulation or distribution was clearly marked while the movement was in its preparatory stages. Experience showed that every well planned and well executed campaign in the market had three stages:

First, in the case of an upward movement, the accumulation would appear and this might run several weeks or months.

Next, would be the marking up stage, where the stock was forced upward by either bullish news or aggressive buying until it reached the level where distribution could take place.

The third stage was that of distribution.

Operations for the decline would be the opposite of this cycle.

Very often I found a stock that was being marked up would be driven far beyond the point where a substantial and satisfactory profit could be realized, but as large operators work on an average buying and selling price rather than on a definite figure, in such cases their distribution would take them on the way down. For instance, if a stock was accumulated within a range of from 50 to 60 and the objective average selling point was 80, the issue might be driven up to par and then sold on the way back to 70, so that 80 or better would be the average price received for what was sold.

These points are explained so that the reader may get an idea of how I worked out my problems, my object being to find out or reason out what the large operator did and how he did it; then I could operate in the same way, and probably with greater success. *I saw the great advantage that lay in operating with the mental attitude of the professional trader instead of the attitude of the unsophisticated outsider.*

As previously stated, I first tested out my theory by dealing in fractional lots of stocks. My progress was often halted by unexpected changes in the market, my own tendency to get away from my principles, new developments which caused me to revise many details, and lastly, the necessity for a long series of transactions which would give me a background of experience in this particular way of dealing.

Before I was really successful, I had to practically rebuild my own trading character. One of my greatest difficulties was impatience. Being of an active disposition I could not sit still long enough to allow a big profit to accumulate. In certain periods the brokers made more in commissions than I made in profits. At other times I allowed myself to be influenced by other considerations rather than the action of the market. But finally I overcame most of these faults and began to reap a real benefit from all the thought and self -training I had put into my work.

Without going into all the many details connected with judging the market, which with long practice resolved themselves into a sort of intuition, as explained in *"Studies in Tape Beading,"* it is enough to say that I have since been successful in anticipating what were apparently the turning points in the ten to twenty point swings in the market. And as everyone with a knowledge of the market will understand, success in this line consists in having a greater aggregate profit over the year than the total amount of losses, including commissions, tax and interest charges.

I realize that people in general hold to the illusion that any man who can make money in the stock market should make it by the million. The public seems to think that once you know how to tap the money reservoir all you have to do is let it run. No fallacy could be more misleading.

It is true that a few large traders make spectacular profits at times. But their losses are usually in proportion, and these you never hear of. Those who make millions risk millions— often all they have on a single operation. And they frequently go broke—a condition which I never have experienced in the stock market, simply because I have never allowed myself to get into a vulnerable position. I have withstood several panics without serious losses.

Making a whole lot of money all at once is not my trading objective. I use a comparatively small amount of money in trading—not over five or ten per cent, of my loose capital—because I have no desire to spread myself out too thin, or operate in such a way that any unexpected event will cripple me. I know that there are a number of people who look upon profits as a means of enlarging their market operations. My method is to pull down the profits and invest them in safe income-paying securities, preferably those which have an opportunity to enhance in value.

There is a much greater satisfaction in operating with a small amount of money for various reasons: It makes you more careful, because, having set yourself to the task of realizing a large profit on a limited amount of operating capital, you plan your moves shrewdly and do not take risks such as you would if operating with more money. In the next place you feel that you are risking very little to make considerable. There is vastly more satisfaction in making $10,000 on a $5,000 capital than in making the same amount where $25,000 is employed.

The operations which have been the most gratifying to me are those in which I h^ve taken, at various times, $3,000 and put it into an account in a broker's office where I could get the right kind of service at a time I expected a move of twelve or fifteen points in a certain security. One of my favorite stocks in this respect has always been U. S, Steel with which I have probably had greater success than any other issue. A few years ago, when I was very busily engaged and could not watch the market all day, I used to wait for U. S. Steel to get into position where I expected such a sharp upward or downward move and then I would buy (or sell) 300 shares, placing a three point stop order for protection. Every two points up I would buy another hundred shares, protecting each additional lot with a three-point stop. After the stock had risen about ten points I would discontinue buying. By that time I would have 800 shares. I would take my profit on a further advance or raise the stop order so that I was sure to have at least several thousand dollars profit.

In the particular year that I mentioned above, I did very little trading except for three such campaigns in U. S. Steel, where not more than $3,000 original margin was used in each campaign, but from which my net profit was about $20,000. This is what I call "good trading" because it was done with very limited risk and the profits were large in proportion to the original amount. After the first campaign, the profits were sufficient to supply the capital for the second and third operations.

Now this is not intended to convey that I, or anyone else, can continue to trade indefinitely with uninterrupted success. It merely illustrates one method of operating which has the advantages described. It always reminds me of a war-^ship which, instead of turning its broadside to the enemy, shows only its bow and thus makes much less of a target. Quite a number of men in Wall Street operate in this way.

You don't hear about them, because they don't happen to be publishing magazines or writing books. As an old friend of mine told me a few days ago, speaking of a former member of a New York Stock Exchange firm:

"He is the most successful speculator I ever met. He will watch a stock carefully and when he judges by its action that it is ready for an important move, he will buy perhaps 500 shares. If it goes in his direction he will buy additional lots every point up, but if it should decline two or three points after he has bought it, he will throw it out immediately on the ground that his first judgment was wrong. He has made so much money now that he takes up, and pays for, ten-thousand-share lots of stock, which in itself is evidence of what he has accomplished."

Before I go any further, let me say that not every man is adapted to trading in stocks. In fact, very few are fitted for the work if it is undertaken as an art, a business, a profession, or whatever else you wish to call it. One reason is that most men have a commercial training, and this unfits them for dealing actively in securities. One of the worst traders 1 ever knew was a man who was highly successful in fact, had made a fortune, in real estate. His method was to buy lots on the fringe of the city and sell them out whenever he secured a substantial profit. He applied this method to the stock market. The result was that he bought in all kinds of markets, and very often had to carry securities for months or years before he could get out. He did not realize that the tendency might change its course several times a year, and there are cross currents and counter currents which must be allowed for, which are not present in real estate.

The merchant who buys his goods wholesale, knowing that there is an established market which will yield him perhaps a ten per cent, profit after overhead and selling expenses, is also handicapped when he comes to Wall Street. One reason is that he is accustomed to buying before he sells, *whereas a man who is trading in securities should able, ready and willing to sell short with as great facility as if buying for long account.* The merchant is familiar with the market in his own field. He judges that market by the supply and demand, and his purchases are made accordingly; but in Wall Street he does not study supply and demand because it is a very technical subject and requires close attention for a number of years before one can master it. Even then, the best and most experienced traders have their bad times and their unfortunate seasons when the character of the market becomes too puzzling or for some reason their judgment is not up to par.

The manufacturer sells short when he takes orders for goods he has not yet manufactured. He sees orders for these goods piling up and thereupon covers his short transactions by purchasing the raw material and eventually manufacturing and delivering the finished goods; but when he enters the business of buying and selling securities, selling short is the last thing he wants to do.

From this it will be seen that special training is necessary if one is to avoid joining the ranks of those who have met the enemy and have been defeated.

Bear in mind that I am referring to the business of active trading and not to the business of investing successfully, which is an entirely different proposition, as will be described later.

Some of the principles which I have found to be advantageous in trading are as follows:

THE MAIN FACTOR IS THE TREND. If you work in harmony with the trend of the market, your-chances for success are three or four times what they would be if you buck the trend. That is, if you buy in a bull market, the trend will, under ordinary circumstances, give you a profit; but if the trend of the market is downward, and you take a long position, the only way you can get out is on the incidental rally. This brief statement covers the point about as well as could be done in many chapters.

RISK SHOULD ALMOST INVARIABLY BE LIMITED. Not only the experience of those whose trading I have observed but my own experience proves that whenever one departs from this general principle he is inviting serious losses. The best way to limit your risk is to form a habit of placing two- or three-point stops behind any trade which is made for the purpose of deriving a profit from the fluctuations. Harriman contended three-eights of a point, or one point, was enough; but of course he was originally a trader on the floor of the Stock Exchange. The most successful traders have followed this rule and its importance cannot be overestimated.

ANTICIPATED PROFITS SHOULD BE AT LEAST THREE OR FOUR TIMES THE AMOUNT OF THE RISK. It must be expected that a percentage of your transactions will show a loss. The trader should aim to have such large profits on his successful trades that the losses and other expenses will still leave him something to the good. Profits can often be protected by moving stop orders up or by selling one-half of the commitment in order to mark down the cost of the remaining half. Many articles on this subject have appeared in past volumes of *The Magazine of Wall Street.*

ONE SHOULD BE ABLE TO DEAL FREELY ON BOTH SIDES OF THE MARKET. Any one who is unable to do this had better become an investor instead of a trader, buying in panics or on big declines such securities as appear to be selling below their intrinsic value.

Dealings Should Be in the Active Stocks. In order to make a profit, a stock must move. A great deal of money and many opportunities are lost by traders who keep themselves tied up in stocks which are sluggish in their action. In a commercial line you would not carry goods on your shelves indefinitely—you would keep your stock moving. In trading, keep on moving stocks!

You Should Either Make a Business of Trading or Else Not Try to Be a Trader. You cannot be successful at trading any more than you can be at mining, manufacturing, doctoring or anything else, unless you are trained for it. And by "training" I do not mean an occasional dab. Incidentally, unless you are peculiarly adapted to the business you had better become an intelligent investor instead of an unintelligent trader.

E. H. HARRIMAN

One of his principles was "I am not interested in ten per cent.; I want something that will grow."

III.
WHY I BUY CERTAIN STOCKS AND BONDS

THERE is an old adage, "It is easier to make money than to keep it." I not only aim to make money, but to keep it and make it grow.

The latter is often the biggest problem of all. It involves something like defensive trench warfare. There is your back line of solid investments, bought principally for income and whatever increase in principal may result. In front of these is your second line of defense against poverty and old age, consisting of securities bought for income and profit. Out in front is your line of speculative securities which you handle so as to gain further ground, without losing your hold on your second and third line of defenses.

In choosing the better grade of securities I give serious consideration to such especially advantageous issues as equipment notes. These are known as a "pawn broker's security" because they are generally issued to secure a purchase of locomotives and cars on which a payment of ten or twenty per cent, is made by a railroad company. The balance of the obligation is paid off in annual installments covering ten, fifteen or twenty years. As the obligation is thus annually reduced, the security for the remaining equipment grows 'larger and larger each year, in proportion to the indebtedness, so that toward the end of the equipment trust period the amount of the security in the shape of rolling stock increases to many hundred per cent, of the amount remaining to be paid. Equipment trusts are, therefore, to be regarded as prime investment mediums.

In spite of the many difficulties surrounding the construction and development of American railroads, I believe there is scarcely an instance where equipment bonds have been defaulted upon. Such issues are therefore well adapted to the final protection of one's investment stronghold.

Another line of income-bearing securities which I frequently favor may be found in the numerous issues of short term notes, which are excellent mediums for funds that are being put aside for specific purposes, and which will be required on a definite date. I find that their yield is often more liberal than one would expect, considering the character of the companies issuing these notes and the yield of their other securities. Due to the vagaries of the investment market, I have often picked up bargains in notes, especially those which were convertible into other securities. But one must be very careful in the selection of these, as any question as to a company being able to meet its obligations will come to the surface as the time approaches for the maturity of its short term notes.

When it comes to safe bond investments, I generally favor properties whose promise to pay is absolutely sound, but whose security is beyond question, and if possible I like, in addition, large equities such as treasury assets, as in the case of Union Pacific, oil lands, and other subsidiaries as in the case of Southern Pacific, holdings in affiliated railroad systems, as in the Pennsylvania Railroad treasury, etc.

My object in making money in securities is to have more money to invest. When I make money in the market, I don't look upon it is a means of trading in a larger way, but I consider the income that money will produce—not only the immediate income, but what in addition might be yielded from the increase in the principal if the original money is properly invested.

Long ago, for the most part, I adopted Harriman's principle which was: "I am not interested in 10 per cent. I want something that will grow." And so, in selecting securities, I try in the main to pick out those which have not small but great possibilities.

There are various kinds of investors. Some want the highest grade bonds even though the income return is small. Others want preferred stocks which yield from 6% to 8 per cent, and which, unlike bonds, never come due, and pay their dividends indefinitely, if properly selected! Next come those investors who are willing to buy the best class of common stocks in an endeavor not only to secure dividends but to see their principal enhance in value, and are satisfied with a moderate profit.

With the major part of my available funds, I invest in a somewhat different way, realizing that the number of years in which a man may operate successfully is limited. I want to put as much money as I can into investment channels where it will grow rapidly so that I can put the increment to work again on the same basis.

Being close to the seat of operations in the financial district I see too many opportunities for profitable investment and increase in principal to allow any substantial amount of money to remain idle. While I always have a certain amount of money in high grade investments, I have not reached the age or the stage where I think more of income than of increase in principal value. As I grow older, no doubt the proportion of securities bought for income will increase, but at age 46, as the insurance companies say, I consider that, in my particular case, it is too early for me to develop into a chronic coupon clipper.

High grade securities and coupons are, however, the proper medium for the majority of those who read this book—emphatically for those who are not experts in distinguishing real investments and real opportunities. They should remain in the income-only stage, so far as most of their funds are concerned.

While there are seasons particularly advantageous for certain operations in the security market, and while these seasons may often seem a long time in coming, one has only to look up the record of the fluctuations in high grade bonds to know that once in a great while they are on the bargain counter. December, 1919, was one of those times, and I was not blind to the fact. It is seldom, indeed, that one can secure the old line, railway bonds, safe beyond question, at such prices as were obtainable then, and with such a long term of years to maturity. In the belief that my investor readers may be interested in knowing what factors convinced me that bonds were "too low" at that time, I append an analysis of the financial situation as I then wrote it, and which was published in the columns of *The Magazine of Wall Street.*

"While it is always time to buy securities for income only, when they can be had at a rate satisfactory to the buyer, this appears to be a time of times, and unless another world cataclysm should occur, a duplicate of this situation may not be seen for another ten or twenty years.

"In former years the railroads were about the only mediums for safe bond investments; but we today have a large variety of industrial and other kinds of mortgages which afford equal if not greater safety, and in many cases a larger net return.

"These are times when a man is justified in loading up with these high grade securities, that is, buying twice as many as he wants to keep permanently. This he can readily do by purchasing and paying for only half of the quantity he buys, carrying the securities in his bank, and gradually paying off the balance out Of income. It matters not whether this income arises from these investments or from his business or other outside sources. Any bank with which you have dealt with will be glad to extend this accommodation; in fact, it will increase the bank's respect for your judgment.

"The present time (December, 1919) affords a rare opportunity. Such an operation should yield not only a substantial profit on the extra quantity which you now purchase, but this profit applied to the reduction of the cost of the balance of the bonds which you now acquire will so enhance the net income from the entire operation that the opportunity should by no means be overlooked.

"Never before have high grade bonds, legal for savings banks in New York State, sold so low as late in 1919. A glance over the list shows that many leading issues are selling at from ten to twenty-five points below their high figures of two years ago. Take old line investments like Union Pacific 1st 4s, having twentyseven years to run, netting about 5.25%; Southern Pacific Ref. 4s of 1955, netting 5,45%; Norfolk & Western consolidated 4s, 1996, 5.23%; Louisville & Nashville gold 5s of 1937, 5.09%; Chicago & Northwestern general 3½s of 1987 netting 5.26%; Burlington general 4s of 1958, netting 5.43%. These are all bonds which will recover sharply in price as soon as the money situation definitely changes, and the limit of foreign government emissions has been seen.

"The Union Pacific 4%) bonds of 1947, selling at about 82, are around 18 points under their market price of two years ago, and one only has to await changed conditions to see a bond of this type rise to its natural level. If this should occur in three years, the average increase in value would be 6% per annum, which, added to the nearly 5% current return on the investment should mean an annual return of about 11%. If such an advance should occupy five years, the return would be 8%. These figures spell opportunity."

One field which has attracted me has been bank stocks, and the reasons were very clearly set forth in a series of articles on this subject appearing in *The Magazine of Wall Street.*

In selecting securities of banks and other financial institutions, one is in the same position as the person who is driving an automobile. He has usually three speeds in his gear case. He can travel slowly on the first set of gears, or a little faster on the second set, or very fast on "high." The institution which does an old style banking business may be likened to the first set of gears. It makes progress within a certain radius, but when a bank takes on a trust department, or a close affiliation with a trust company, making the two parts of one institution, it may be regarded as traveling on second speed. But there is still another type of institution which includes both the above and embraces an additional function which in the financial district is a very advantageous one to the stockholder. I refer to a bank which owns or is affiliated with a "Security Company" for the purpose of underwriting and conducting syndicate and investment security operations, which are, of course, very profitable.

I have been buying stocks in a dozen or more New York financial institutions. I put these in the custody of a trust company, separate from any other securities, so that dividends, rights, and stock distributions would all be paid in to this one account and reinvested in the same class of securities. My observation has shown that to secure the greatest benefit from bank stock investments, one should not spend the income derived therefrom, nor sell his rights, nor sell any stock distributions that are given, because these in time generate other melons of the same sort, and this second generation gives birth to successive series of children and grandchildren, which eventually roll up a very substantial amount of both income and principal.

In placing these securities with the trust company for safekeeping and reinvestment, I told the trust officer of the institution that this account would be in debt most of the time, because I would buy ahead of the income and I would expect the trust company to loan whatever moneys were required for that purpose.

During the latter part of 1919 two of these opportunities developed: The Bankers Trust Co. directors recommended an increase in the capital stock from $15,000,000 to $20,000,000, the new stock to be offered to shareholders at a price of $100 per share. This is on the basis of one share of new stock for every three shares of old. Holding shares of Bankers Trust, which cost in the neighborhood of $485 per share, I was entitled to subscribe to new stock at $100, which brought the average cost down to about $389 per share.

In time these new shares will be producing other stock dividends, rights, or cash dividends, so that eventually I may have a considerable amount of Bankers Trust Co. stock. By reinvestment of income in whatever form it is distributed, the cost of this Bankers Trust Co. stock will be reduced to a very low figure.

Another case of this kind appeared not long ago in the form of a notice sent to stockholders of the Chase National Bank, which I purchased at about $675 per share. Stockholders were asked to vote on an increase in the capital stock of the bank from $10,000,000 to $15,000,000, with a proportionate increase in the shares of the Chase Securities Co., which is affiliated with the bank. Holders were to be allowed to subscribe to one new share of the Bank stock and one new share of the Securities Company, for each two old shares thereof held prior to December 26, 1919. The subscription price was $250 for one share of stock of the Bank and one share of stock of the Securities Co. I have no doubt that in time the value of all these shares, viz., the new, which I have bought, and the old which will sell ex-rights, will recover to the price which I paid for the old stock, which was $675 per share. This means that I have faith not only in these and the other banking institutions in which I have become a stockholder, but in the men behind them, and in the future of New York City as the world's banking center.

I estimate that the average return over a period of years, allowing for rights, melons, regular and extra cash distributions, etc., in the leading issues is something over 12% per annum. At this rate, my investment should double itself in a period of something between six and seven years, allowing for the reinvestment of all dividends of every sort in the same class of securities.

The small percentage of failures among banking institutions, now that they are under such rigid control by the Federal authorities, make their securities adapted to the conservative investor who is looking toward income enhancement and safety. My own selection included a larger proportion of shares in those institutions which have security companies attached, because these combine two companies in one, and in all cases they are being conducted with highly profitable results to the shareholders.

This taking a sum of money and planting it in a certain field without drawing down the income, but with intent to profit by its growth, may be followed out to whatever degree the investor desires. It may be begun with one share of one bank stock, or any other kind of stock or bond. It is an investment operation, but it is undertaken for income and profit, not with the idea of deriving or withdrawing that profit, but to make it yield additional sums for investment. It is a great deal like a savings bank account for the man with a small amount of cash, I remember how, with a great deal of pride, I started my first savings account with a five dollar bill (because the bank would not open an account for less), and how much satisfaction I derived from being able to add a few more fives and tens.

The man or woman who is obliged to withdraw his or her interest or, in case of a rainy day, pull down part of the principal, will be handicapped in an operation of this sort, but the object should be to make these deficiencies up when the skies again dear and to keep expenses within bounds so that the additions made annually will rapidly increase the earning power of the principal.

D. L. & W's Tunkhannock Viaduct

Showing the topography over which the Lackawanna has triumphed and typical of the immense property investment the shares represent

IV. UNEARTHING PROFIT OPPORTUNITIES

WHEN I buy bonds and other high grade securities for income and profit, I favor those which for special reasons are well adapted to my purpose.

First, I consider those which are selling below their intrinsic value, based on character of security. In such -a case I do not lay too much stress on the interest return, although in some cases it is large. The question of marketability is important with me, however, because I prefer issues that can be instantly turned into cash. The reason for this is that always I desire always to be in a position to take advantage of a threatened panic or bargain opportunity, and as I watch the market and the general situation very closely, I frequently detect signs of trouble 'way in the distance and prepare for it.

In the case of certain 5% bonds which I hold, these are well secured, earning a big surplus, which for some reason or another is concealed.

Selling around 60, the income is very large if figured to maturity, but in selecting this bond I had my eye more on the probability that the investment public will wake up to its real value and mark its price up twenty or twenty-five points within the next two or three years. In case of an advance to 85 within three years, there would be about $8^{1}/_{3}\%$ profit per annum, to be added to the flat yield of the bond. Such a 5% bond at 60, would net about 8% %, disregarding any re-investment of income. If, on top of this, I realize another $8^{1}/_{3}\%$ in three years, the income plus profit would be $16^{2}/_{3}\%$ per annum.

A class of bond which I hold and always favor, is the convertible. The advantages of convertible bonds have been too often described in past issues of *The Magazine of Wall Street* to necessitate repetition here, but if one would make 3, persistent study of these convertible issues, he would find every year new opportunities for making *growing investments*. Whatever is a little complicated for the average investor is apt to be overlooked and' neglected. To get the best results one should be familiar with the technicalities of many kinds of convertible bonds and the stipulations under which they are issued.* In some cases it does require some figuring to find out just what can be done with these issues.

For my own investment I am seldom attracted to convertible bonds solely from the standpoint of income, but only when I see possibilities in the securities into which they are convertible. In 1918 I bought $100,000 of a certain convertible bond because I saw great future possibilities in the stock into which they were convertible at par. At that time the stock was selling close to the price of the bonds, viz., around 90. Observation of the action of the bonds during the period of weakness in the stock convinced me that the bonds would not decline very much even if the stock were to break ten or fifteen points, because the investment value of the bonds kept them up at a level where the interest return to the investor brought in buying enough to sustain the market price. By purchasing the convertible bonds I would have something that I need not be concerned about, and I was sure that, if the investment public realized the intrinsic

These will be found in "Convertible Bonds," by Rollins, price $3, net-value in the stock, my convertible bonds would follow the stock along up. This is exactly what happened. Sometime later the stock rose twenty-five points and the bonds kept a little above it, until one day the bonds were selling so much higher than the stock that I sold the bonds and bought the stock instead, thus marking down the cost of my bonds by an amount representing the difference between the price of the two securities.

This marking down the cost, by the way, is a very important factor in making investments, I keep it constantly in mind. Every investor should remember that by selling a portion of his holdings at a profit he is reducing the cost of the balance. It is good practice. I will elaborate later.

Naturally, in dealing, as I do, in all kinds of securities, there are quite a number of reasons for my going into a stock in 1913 or 1914 I wrote a series on "Which Kind of a Stock Is Best?" This was done as much for my own information as for my subscribers', and while I am on this subject I should like to say that I take my own medicine. In searching the security market I have a twin purpose, viz., to find investment opportunities for my own money and to tell my subscribers about them. I figure that what is good enough for my subscribers is good enough for me. Ai the same time I wish to say that, I make mistakes at times; so does everybody, no matter how long he has been in the field.

My constant aim is to show my readers, directly or between the lines, how they may be able to judge for themselves. As was written by an author unknown to me: " There are men who will take no initiative on their own responsibility, who will undertake nothing without consulting others as to the feasibility of the schemes and plans they have in view. When a man puts more confidence in another than in himself he is bound to lose all will power and become a mere dependent, awaiting orders as to the course of action. It is impossible for such a man to get along in the world and make a success of his own life. When opportunity comes along he is afraid to seize it without asking his neighbor's opinion.

So what I and my staff try to do is to make our readers think and plan and carry out their campaign in the investment field just as they do in their own business. This was one of my purposes in Writing the series, "Which Kind of a Stock is Best? " As those articles progressed they indicated that the chain store and mail order stocks were, in many respects, better than the other leading groups such as steel, copper, railroad, telephone, etc., the principal reason being that these companies were putting more of their earnings back into their business than any other single group.

And so I bought Sears, "Roebuck & Co., because its history shows that every three or four years a stock dividend is declared. This has been the practice of the company for many years. By this method Sears, Roebuck & Co. keep the cash in their business and use it for healthy and profitable expansion, The stockholder who owns a hundred shares is given twenty-five or thirty-three shares of new stock, which adds to his income without cutting down the working capital of his company. This twenty-five or thirty-three shares additional will, in ensuing years, probably yield another six or eleven shares and these, in turn, will eventually breed other little stock dividends, all of which, added to the original shares, should in time double the quantity of an investor's holdings, without any further investment of cash by him.

The purchase of a stock like Delaware, Lackawanna & Western Railroad is one which I made for an entirely different reason. Its dividend yield did not attract me, but having been over the property I realized what an enormous amount had been expended on improvements of far-reaching importance. One official is quoted as saying that they have invested, in road and and equipment, money for expenditures that could easily have been put off for twenty or twenty-five years. You may say, "That is a strange reason for investing in a railroad stock when the railroad situation is so unfavorable." But let me tell you that when you buy into a company like that, with enormous equities buried as a result of successful operations in the past, you will eventually see a still greater return, because one of these days the railroads, including Lackawanna, will again come into their own.

Lackawanna, at the end of 1918, had a profit and loss surplus of $57,247,984 against a total outstanding stock of $42,277,000. In June, 1909, it declared a cash dividend of 50% out of its surplus, and a stock dividend of 15%. In November, 1911, it declared a stock dividend of 35%, payable in stock of the Lackawanna railroad of New Jersey. The system is only 980 miles long, but it is the Croesus among railroads. From 1906 to the present time, 160 is the lowest it has sold. In May, 1919 it touched 217. Hence, when in October, 1919, I saw it decline to around 180 on a threatened coal strike, I considered it cheap, and if it should decline further I would regard it as a greater bargain.

Wall Street history shows that securities more often reach their low point when some danger or disaster is *threatened,* than upon the actual occurrence of these incidents, and the reason the low point is made just prior to, or at the time the event actually occurs, is: By that time every one who is subject to fear-of-what-will-happen, has sold out. When the thing does happen or is prevented, there is no more liquidation, and the price rallies on the short interest, or else on the investment demand created by the improved situation.

It was for these reasons that I bought Delaware, Lackawanna & Western railroad Company's stock.

Speaking of high priced stocks like Sears, Roebuck, Lackawanna and others, there is a very important reason why these are cheaper than the very low-priced stocks. Many of the shares selling in the 10 's, 20 's and 30 's represent very little earning power. In many cases only one or two per cent, is being earned on the latter issues, with little or no prospect of dividends. Stocks paying 5 to 8% range from $60 to $100 per share. On this basis a stock paying 1% could be worth from $12 to $20. This would indicate that a non-dividend payer is worth somewhere between nothing and $12. Everything above that is hope capitalized.

Yet we have seen many non-dividend payers sell at all sorts of prices before their initial declaration. American Can, for example, sold not long ago at 68 without ever having paid a dividend. Brooklyn Rapid Transit, in 1899, sold, as a non-dividend payer, at 137; it did not make its first dividend disbursement for ten years after that.

But take the stocks selling at $200 to $400 per share and upward, and in normal times you generally find intrinsic values, future prospects, or earning power, or all combined, which justify these prices and more. Most of the very high priced stocks have hidden equities which may not benefit the stockholders right away, but which are working for them just the same. These factors may not interest the man who is long today and short tomorrow, but they do interest the permanent investor who has his eye on the development of the corporation and the future growth of the various industries and the country in general. That is why I favor high-priced stocks rather than very low-priced speculative issues.

V. SOME EXPERIENCES IN MINING STOCKS

THE investor who always chooses securities of companies who constantly put money back into their properties, will scarcely ever go wrong, but he must be constantly on the alert to notice any change in policy due to altered conditions, or to control of the property getting into other hands. The New York, New Haven & Hartford Railroad was formerly an example of progressive and conservative management and for many decades was considered a high grade investment. But the time came when a policy of expansion brought the New Haven to grief. Of this there were many signs, especially when the persistent character of the liquidation indicated that something was wrong.

Carnegie said, "Put all your eggs in one basket and watch the basket." I would distribute my eggs and watch all of the baskets.

Never get married to a security. You may have it salted down, but there is no reason why you shouldn't freshen up your list every once in a while by going over and carefully considering what you hold and whether something else wouldn't work to better advantage for you. I find I get best results by considering each investment a separate little business enterprise. When I buy a security I figure that while as a bondholder I am a creditor and my money is secured this is not true when I become a stockholder. That makes me a partner in the enterprise and as such I want to be a live partner, not a dead one; for if I don't look after my own interests nobody else will.

That explains one reason why I like to be associated in partnership with people who are high class in every respect—because I know that they are not lying awake nights planning ways to do me or the other stockholders out of our money. Possibly no corporation head is beyond criticism, but anyone who puts his dollars into corporations like U. S. Steel, Bethlehem Steel, General Motors, General Electric and other leaders in industry and finance may rest assured that these companies are being run by the highest type of industrial captains who are intent upon making their enterprises profitable to the hundreds of thousands of big and little stockholders.

"Choose your company" is therefore a good precept for the investor.

There used to be a gang of highwaymen operating here in the Street and using the leading railroad and industrial shares as the scissors by which they parted the public from its money, but that day is rapidly passing. Leaders in finance learned long ago that they could make more money by the square deal than in any other manner. Nevertheless, I find that it pays to be sceptical until you are convinced by the past record of those in the management that they are working in your interest and not in their own.

For my own benefit, as well as that of every reader of *The Magazine of Wall Street*, I am investigating these essential factors more than ever before. It is not enough for one to know that a certain development is indicated by the surface facts and conditions—I want to get down into the root of things and find out why. For this reason I employ investigators, lawyers, mining and oil engineers. I send people to different parts of the country to get the local color and all the angles on a proposition.

After employing one engineer I sometimes send another to check him up. It might cost a few thousand dollars, but when you are putting real money into an enterprise you cannot be too sure, nor investigate too thoroughly. Not long ago I had two mining enterprises put up to me, which on a cursory examination looked good. It cost me two thousand dollars to have these properties examined, and on the engineer's reports I turned them down. In one case the mine has turned out better than was first represented to me. Either or both of these properties might develop into big mining enterprises, but taking all the facts into consideration I concluded they were not good enough for me to invest in.

While an engineer's report is by no means the last word on a property, it is a hundred times better to have an expert opinion than to take your own or some other layman's view; yet the peculiar part of mining is that even though the most eminent engineers may give an adverse report on a property, it may eventually fool them.

Mining has a great fascination for me. In fact, what came out of the ground was always of peculiar interest to numerous members of the Wyckoff family. The original Wyckoff, after landing in New York in the early sixteen hundreds, had charge of Peter Stuyvesant's estate, which was located in downtown New York, where the Hudson Terminal Building now stands. His descendant, my grandfather, who organized the Hanover Fire Insurance Co., and was one of the original interests in the Hanover National Bank, was also deeply interested in mining. He invented a separation process back in the fifties and successfully mined gold in the State of Virginia before and during the Civil War near where the Battle of the Wilderness was fought.

If I had my business career to plan over again, I would be inclined to favor mining engineering, for it is an interesting profession; but in visiting numerous mining properties and watching the methods of engineers and the difficult conditions which often prevail in the different mines, I can readily see how Old Mother Earth can fool the best of them. For that reason I never go into a mining enterprise unless I am prepared to lose every cent I put into it.

But there are many ways in which even a layman can check up such an imposing person as the mining engineer. I have made considerable money in mining stocks, and I expect to make a great deal more because I have learned a lot thus far and will use what knowledge I have to better advantage in the future.

First of all, I want to know who are the interests behind the mine—whose dollars are alongside of mine ? Have they a record for successfully developing other mining enterprises? What mistakes have they made? Were they fooled themselves or did they fool the stockholders—which or both? Along what line is the development work now proceeding? Is the company properly financed? What is the character and reputation of the engineer who is guiding the development work? Is the metal or mineral which they are producing such that an advantageous market is afforded now and at all times? If it is a gold, silver or copper mine, what is the outlook for those metals? Are future conditions so shaping themselves that the mine can be regarded as more or less of a manufacturing and therefore an investment proposition? Is the nature of the ore such that it will peter out within a few years or is there a certain deposit of ascertainable value which can be diamond-drilled and its value estimated? Under these conditions, what is the probable life of the mine and the estimated profit per share during that period? These and dozens of other questions are what I ask myself and others before putting my money into a property.

Some mines are highly speculative; some are at or approaching the investment stage. My problem is to get aboard the best of them before they get to a stage where the cream is all off. In other words, I want some of the cream, and in order to-get it I frequently have to go in early and sit in for a long time before the skimming process can be accomplished.

Sometimes I go into a mining stock in order to derive a profit from the fluctuations in the market price, and other times to get my profit out of the ground. In order to illustrate this point I will explain an operation in Magma Copper, which stock I have held in substantial quantity for over four years.

I was coming downtown one-day when a friend whom I met told me there was "something doing" in Magma, and suggested that I watch it. I did watch it, and saw that careful buying was proceeding. (I always lay more stress on the action of the market than on what anybody says.) As' I remember, the stock originally came out at about $12 per share, rose to $18, then sold off to around $15. When he told me this it was up to $20, indicating that new influences were at work.

I decided to buy 200 shares and await further developments. The price hung around the same figure for a day or two, when suddenly my broker called me up and said Magma was 21 bid, whereupon I immediately gave him an order to buy 500 shares at the market. He had to pay 22 for some of it. I then bought another 500 shares, which cost me a point or so higher. As I always like to buy something that is "hard to purchase," the action of this stock pleased me very much, especially as it closed that night around 28 or 29.

Then I set out to find what it was all about, and I learned that the character of the ore in Magma had been discovered to be such that if it was present in any great quantity the mine would be one of the most important in this country, for insiders would then consider it worth $200 per share. So I told my friends about it.

No doubt the bucket shops were heavily short of this stock, because when the urgent buying continued, the price rose rapidly, until in about three weeks it sold at 69, and I had about $55,000 profit on my 1,200 shares.

Did I take this profit! I did not. I did not go into it for that amount of money. Have I been joshed about not taking it during the time the stock has wiggled back and forth between 25 and 55 for the last four years? I have. Why did I not take it? I'll tell you: Because when I bought that stock I resolved that more money was to be made out of the mine than out of the fluctuations—unless someone was lying. And following my usual resolution to be prepared for the loss of whatever I put into any mine, I made up my mind to sit with my $23,000 investment in Magma until it proved to be either a fake or a bonanza.

It has proved to be a bonanza, and although the stock is today selling for only one-half of its high price of 69, I not only have the same opinion of its future as was indicated in 1915, but I have many, many more reasons, for believing in the soundness of the enterprise.

Magma Copper Company is capitalized at $1,500,000 authorized, and $1,200,000 outstanding stock of $5 par value. There being only 240,000 shares, a price of 35 represents a market value of $8,400,000. The leading interest is Col. Wilzam B. Thompson, who, in the last twelve or fifteen years, has made more millions in mining securities than any other man in Wall Street.

Ever since the real value of the property was discovered Mr. Thompson and his friends have been steadily accumulating Magma, until now, out of the 240,000 shares, there are not more than

20,000 shares in the hands of the public. How do I know this? Because I have gone to very great trouble and expense to check it up from various angles. I am not taking anybody's word; I have got at the *facts*, not only from a Wall Street point of view. A few months ago I visited the property, and with my mining engineer went down to the 1,400-foot level. I saw 40% to 60% bornite on all sides of me in some of the tunnels and cross-cuts.

The property is being developed on a tremendous scale, and now that its new shaft has been completed, it is ready for quantity production. Its silver and gold values so reduce the cost of its copper that it is one of the lowest priced producers in this country today. And down below there is a world of ore.

Those who know Colonel Thompson best say he will never sell his Magma. For my part, I intend to wait until I see him start to distribute, and then they can have mine.

Carping critics will say, "He's trying to boost Magma, so he can sell it." Let them carp. I don't care whether anyone who reads this buys Magma or not. It makes no difference either to Colonel Thompson, to me, or to my friends and subscribers who have bought the stock on the strength of what they have read in *The Magazine*, and who hold most of the 20,000 shares to which I have referred. All I wish to say to them is: Hold it, and you won't be sorry. As for professional parasites and self-appointed critics, let me call their attention to the fact that I talk, write, investigate, trade and invest in nearly all securities on the New York Stock Exchange and outside at one time or another. Hence, criticisms may as well be prepared in advance and arranged alphabetically for easy and prompt access when required.

This experience in Magma illustrates the advantage of thoroughly investigating and then sticking to your holdings like grim death, or until something occurs which, for a definite reason, causes you to change your position. I do not claim that the paper profit in Magma thus far is any criterion, but I wish to emphasize the importance of making a resolution in connection with investment or speculative transactions and basing that resolution on sound premises—making of them a sort of statistical rock upon which you may place your feet and stand there indefinitely.

Lots of people have said, "Why didn't you sell out and buy back cheaper?" Personally, I have never made any money by trading backward, by which I refer to the hind-sight which is so frequently flourished in Wall Street as an indication that the flourisher is blessed with an acute foresight.

Had I sold at the high price, I could of course have bought back on a scale down, or a lower figure, then re-sold and re-bought, but as I have said, I was not in that kind of an operation, although it took considerable strength of purpose to resist at times. Ore in the ground, when combined with first-class management, ample capital and big personal commitments on the part of those who are running the property, is about as safe as money in the bank; but it must be the right kind of ore and in such quantity that it will yield a very large return in proportion to the original investment.

Elsewhere the reader will find reference to the difficulty in waiting for a big profit, but in the main people have less trouble with their patience when they face a large loss. There is one way in which most of this difficulty can be overcome, and that is by carefully assembling the facts when you enter a commitment and continually checking up all along the line for the entire time that you hold it. There is no need for guess-work, if one will take the trouble. It is merely a question of how much labor and expense you are willing to go to in order to make your investment successful.

We succeed in proportion to the amount of energy and enterprise we use in going after results. Success is not for the man who is willing to sit down and wait for something to fall into his lap.

It is poor policy, I find, to wait for Opportunity to knock at your door, I train my ear so that I can hear Opportunity coming down the street long before it reaches my door. When Opportunity knocks, I try to reach out, grab Opportunity by the collar and yank it in.

JOHN D. ROCKFELLER

Whose fortune of nearly one billion dollars represents investments, for the greater part, in the necessities or near-necessities of life.

VI.
THE FUNDAMENTALS OF SUCCESSFUL INVESTING

ONE of the most important considerations when making an investment is to understand the nature and condition of the industry which that security represents. Look over the mediums which John D. Rockefeller and others of his family select, and you will find that they are mostly in the necessities of life—oil, gas, food or other near necessities, such as iron, steel, harvesting machinery, etc. These are branches of endeavor in which there is an already created and continual demand—human need of fuel, light, eatables, or materials necessary to produce them. It is a good point to bear in mind.

As I get deeper and deeper into this problem of making money in securities, and then making the securities make more money, new avenues for thought, research and investigation are constantly developing. Of late I have been more than ever impressed with the importance of understanding the present condition and future tendency of the industries represented by the multitudinous corporations whose shares are listed or unlisted in New York and elsewhere. It was for this reason that I established in *The Magazine of Wall Street* a department known as Trade Tendencies. This feature is worthy of careful study.

While in former years I usually began with a consideration of the trend of the market, and then passed to the choice of security, I now line the factors up in the following order:

(1) Long trend of the market.

(2) Nature* and tendency of the industry.

(3) Trend of the selected company's affairs (toward .improvement or contrary).

(4) Character and reputation of the management.

(5) Financial position and earning power.

(6) Position in relation to the intermediate, i. e., the thirty to sixty-day swings.

When all of the above prove up to my satisfaction I feel safe in making an investment.

Of course, there are other considerations, but these are the most important.

Practically everyone agrees, and I have proved in another series of articles, how vitally important it is to know the long trend of the market. This is the compass by which all courses should be steered. It is so fundamental that there is a little ground for discussion, but I may say that it is one of the main points in successful investment. The reason is that even when a purchase is not well-timed, it is likely to show a profit at sometime or other if the broad general tendency of prices be upward. Even poor weak stocks advance to some extent in a bull market. On the contrary, if a person buys a stock in a bear market, he is likely to have to carry it a very long while. If it be in a weak financial position, he may have to see it through a receivership, or he may decide to sell out at a big loss in order to save what little remains. From this it will be seen how important is knowledge of the long trend.

Suppose I have decided that the automobile industry is in a very sound, prosperous and promising condition, and I am considering an investment in one of the best of the automobile companies' shares. I would not feel justified in making this investment unless satisfied that the long trend of the market is upward. The action of the market discounts the business situation six months to a year in advance; prices of stocks point farther ahead than any individual can see, and because these prices represent the combined or composite opinion of the millions of people who are dealing in securities. They express themselves by their purchases and sales; hence a study of the tendency of the general market and of individual stocks is a study of the minds of men.

Therefore, when I decide that the automobile industry is in a favorable position, and that the long trend of the market is upward, I set about to select the company engaged in that industry; then I determine (a) whether the tendency of its business is toward improvement or to the contrary; (b) character and reputation of the management; (c) financial position and earning power; (d) position of the stock or bond in relation to the general market and its position in the intermediate swings (if it be a stock) represented by the thirty to sixty-day movements in prices.

It is not claimed that I go through any set formulas, but this is the general plan of reasoning which I follow, and which, through long association with the various kinds of market securities, financial statements, management, and periodical swings in prices has become almost instinctive, so that it takes me only a short time to make up my mind that a proposition measures up to my requirements.

At the beginning, of course, I had to sit down like anybody else and pore over a mass of data and statistics and look up records just as a lawyer, doctor, or anyone else has to do when he first begins to practice. But trading and investing is like any other pursuit—the longer you stay at it the more technique you acquire, and anybody who thinks he knows of a shortcut that will not involve "sweat of the brow" is sadly mistaken.

Pertaining to the matter of condition and outlook for the industry in which I might be considering a venture, I want to show how it should take precedence over many other factors which are included in the examination of a contemplated investment. When I first came down to Wall Street, there was practically only one industry represented on the New York Stock Exchange—that of railroading. Everything revolved around the state of the crops, because wheat, corn, oats and other crops were the country's mainstay, and most of the speculative campaigns by large operators like Gould, Keene, Philip Armour, Deacon White and others, started with the crop outlook as the base.

That condition has changed. We have many hundreds of industries represented by the listed and unlisted securities that are now freely dealt in by investors, and this list is being added to every week. So, while the railroad stocks are still a factor, there are more oils than rails and a great many more motors than there used to be. All these groups are subject to various influences which affect their respective industries, and in many cases their industries are so intertwined that prosperity or depression in some is bound to bring about a similar condition in others.

The automobile industry is a striking example of this. If, as one high official has stated, there is a latent demand for two million automobiles, it means that there exists a like possibility of expansion in the rubber tire, steel and oil industries. Another instance is found in the rails. The roads having been handed back to their owners, once their financial position and earning power is assured, there will immediately spring up an unprecedented demand for railway equipment. This in turn would favorably affect the steel industry, because the railroads are such very large consumers of rails and other equipment requiring the use of steel.

Then comes the secondary consideration of the effect of prosperity in these lines upon other industries. Included in automobile manufacture must be literally hundreds of allied lines such as concerns making bodies, tops, radiators, motors, wheels, etc., now that the indirect effect of a prosperous condition in the automobile trade is disseminated through thousands of different channels.

The two factors above named have a still greater influence upon the spending power of the millions whose earnings are kept at a high level by reason of the demand for labor and materials, and what is known as the spending power of the public runs into thousands of trade avenues, resulting in a great stimulation of all lines of industry.

Perhaps I have got away from my subject a little, but it is interesting to follow a thought towards its logical conclusion.

The above condition therefore brings about, directly and indirectly, a stimulation of various lines, while in other industries, working under adverse conditions, the effect is contrary; hence we must conclude that there are numerous tendencies going on in the market all the time, some being reflected by higher prices for these groups of securities, while prices of other groups are declining. This will make clear why it is so important to study the various lines of business in order to choose, by a process of elimination, those which are likely to show the best results, even if conditions in other lines are somewhat unfavorable. I have seen cases where the progress of a certain industry more than offset the declining tendency of the general market, resulting in certain stocks going up while most others were going steadily downward. When I can make an investment in which the condition of that trade is ideal, and when the long trend of the market is strongly upward, with all the above-named factors satisfactory, I feel rather certain that the outcome will be profitable.

These points being settled, the next step is to decide what stock in that industry is in the best position as regards earning power and financial strength, character and reputation of management, etc. From an investment standpoint the above factors should dominate, but from a speculative standpoint, the matter of technical position would have almost equal weight.

In selecting a stock for income and profit, or choosing one which I buy primarily for profit, I always like to choose the one which will make the greatest amount of money for me in the shortest length of time. This is where a study of technical position comes in. A certain stock may look good to me because it has risen from 100 to 150 and then reacted under an assault by the bears (but without any especial change in its fundamental position, outlook or earning power) to a price of 110. If it shows at that level strong resistance to pressure, I would much rather buy it than some stock which was still in the range of distribution after being marked up 40 or 50 points and made very active around the top. These are but simple examples of a study of the action of different stocks and some of my reasons for choosing one rather than the other after giving due weight to all the other factors in the case.

It is strange how people will continue to ignore the important elements just referred to. Probably it is because they do not understand the operations that underlie the fluctuations in securities and which are responsible for many of their movements. I refer to the campaigns mapped out and carried out by pools consisting of groups of a few or many men who look far ahead and observe the approach of a situation which will enable them to buy or sell to advantage.

As Charles H. Dow used to say: "The public rarely sees values until they are pointed out," —which means that the public does not lead, but is led in speculation. It rarely acts until it is told to act, or until action of some sort is suggested by a bit of verbal information, a market letter, etc.

But there is another kind of suggestion which is the most potent in its influence on the public, and that is the action of the market itself. A rising price for a stock suggests still higher prices and declining quotations bear the inference that prices are 'going lower. Pools work on this weakness, which is due to ignorance on the part of the public. They accumulate a stock without advancing its price; then, when market conditions are favorable, they bid the stock up. This excites public buying, because people always want to get in on something that is "going up." Vice versa, groups will often try to depress a stock, counting on the public's support when the issue begins to decline.

It long ago occurred to me that success in the security market demanded an understanding of the operations of those who were most influential, because these interests had been studying the business and operating in the market for many years and were therefore experts. It was sound reasoning to suppose that a knowledge of the principles which they used in their market operations would enable one to detect their thumbprints on the tape and to follow with pleasure and profit.

Large interests are practically always in the market. They usually have their scale orders in on both sides so that they buy on declines and sell on rallies. They always have money with which to buy on declines, because they sell on the rallies. They thus realize a profit as well as supply funds for the next decline. If the public would learn to do this, there would be fewer stock market fatalities.

It is difficult to over-emphasize the importance of studying the technical position, particularly when making a speculative commitment. Many people may say, "What is a weak or a strong technical position?" My reply is, in brief, that a stock is in a weak technical position on the bull side when it has been purchased and is held by a large number of outside speculators; when most of these are looking for a profit; when the price of the stock has advanced to a point where no further buying can be stimulated for the time being. It stands to reason that when buying power is exhausted a stock must decline, no matter how strong its finances, management or earning power.

On the other hand, a stock is in a weak technical position on the short side when the bears have exhausted their ammunition by selling all they can afford and when the buying power of investment and speculative purchasers is such that it resists the pressure of the bears; in other words, when demand overcomes supply. The weakness in such a position is found in the fact that all those who are short are potential bulls; they must, sooner or later, cover their commitments in order to close their trades. They do not wish to remain short indefinitely. It is a well-known fact that bears have less courage than bulls, and they are often obliged to buy at higher prices because the technical position becomes so strong that they cannot force the price lower. Bears, after they have sold short, are an element of strength, not of weakness.

Much could be written on this subject, which, while far from being an exact science because of the numerous and changing influences that are being thrown into the market at almost every moment, is a study which well warrants the attention of every investor and trader. The old adage "well bought is half sold" should always be borne in mind, and while this study of the technical position is a point which people get around to last, one's security market education is not complete without it, nor can it be mastered without patient study, long experience and practice.

There are many men in Wall Street and throughout the country who make a practice of taking profits in accordance with their ideas of proportion, something like this: They say, "Fifty points is a big profit, even if it is on a small lot of stock? therefore, I will take it." Others say to themselves, "I have a profit of a hundred per cent on my investment and that's good enough. I will let someone else have the rest." In the case of American Graphophone, I followed a different rule. The number of points, or the percentage of profit, did not influence me. The fluctuations were interesting, but whether the stock went up or down, I decided to wait for it to reach a certain point before I would take profits. This meant the point where the insiders began to sell.

VII. THE STORY OF A LITTLE ODD LOT

IN previous articles I have referred to the importance of a thorough understanding of the industry represented by the security in which you have decided to invest. One cannot place too much emphasis on this point. Some people, when they look at the list of securities quoted in the dailies, do not know whether the abbreviated titles refer to railroads, industrials, or billy-goats. But they ought to know and especially should they be acquainted with the history, finances and character of management of their chosen enterprises.

For a long time I have been familiar with the history and development of the phonograph industry, and have made calculations as to its future trend. For many years it was largely monopolized through the protection of patents which some people disputed but which were at any rate effective. And so when in February, 1919, 1 was having lunch with a friend, and he told me something important was likely to come out of the approaching-meeting of the American (now Columbia) Graphophone Company, I knew that back of any immediate development in that company's affairs there was a solid foundation for what might occur.

We were discussing how the millions of soldiers who went to the war were coming back music-crazy, and how their experiences abroad and in American camps proved to them the value of the phonograph in the home; how people who never before could afford such luxuries were now able to buy, resulting in an unprecedented demand for both machines and records.

"I understand," said my friend, "that the announcement to follow the Columbia meeting is likely to put the stock to 150."

As the issue was then selling around 135 I did not pay much attention to it, and had almost forgotten the incident when one morning, coming down to the office, I noticed in my newspaper a small announcement to the effect that the Columbia directors had declared a dividend of $2.50 per share in cash and one-twentieth of a share in stock. Elsewhere in the paper, among the obscure news items, it was suggested that it would be the policy of the Graphophone Company in future to disburse a certain amount of cash every quarter and a small stock dividend as well. Both the official announcement and the small news item were couched in such modest terms that the significance thereof did not appear on the surface.

But a little mental calculation worked out like this: $2.50 per share per quarter meant $10 a year. One-twentieth of a share per quarter was four-twentieths, or one-fifth of a share per annum. At the market price of the stock, 135, this one-fifth of a share equals $27 per share per annum, or a total of $37 per share—counting cash and value of stock—dividend. Conclusion: The price should advance from $200 to $300 per share, dependent upon how certain the regularity of the stock dividends intended to be paid.

Upon reaching the office I phoned the company's headquarters and found that the management planned to declare these quarterly stock dividends at the one-twentieth rate indefinitely, so I started to invest at least $15,000 in American Graphophone common at the market price. Evidently other people were awake to what that little announcement meant, for there were lots of buyers and few, if any, sellers. I finally succeeded in buying two twenty share lots, averaging 164 1/4, and the next that was offered to me was around 179. As this was a long way from the price at which I started to buy, and I didn't like to bid up against so much competition, I decided to give the forty shares to my wife and to see what I could do for her with the little odd lot. Soon the price was 180, then 200 bid, with hardly any transaction in the meantime.

These forty shares of stock cost $6,575, which, while not much of an investment, had great possibilities, considering its size, as I will show. It was not my first transaction in Graphophone, for I had made considerable money in it on previous occasions, buying it around 70, selling at 135, re-buying around 110, and carrying it up to 160. Considering these transactions, the forty shares cost me much less than nothing.

About five years ago *The Magazine of Wall Street* published an article on the phonograph industry, which showed it to be in a very prosperous condition with an outlook that was exceptionally promising, A certain New York stock broker, knowing that the stock of the old American Graphophone Company had been well distributed many years before, and that control was to be had in the open market, went to Wilmington, Del., and succeeded in obtaining a fifteenminute interview with the du Pont interests. The upshot of this was that the du Fonts acquired control, buying the stock from below par up to nearly $200 per share for the last of their stock.

Then began a period of development and expansion under the new and more progressive management. In consequence, the company had made very great strides in the last few years. During this time the stock, which had reached 196 or thereabouts, gradually declined, until in the summer of 1918 it was selling around $50 per share. Somewhere between that level and the 135 figure which prevailed when my attention was again called to it, those in control evidently saw an opportunity to "put it over big," just as they had in General Motors and other large corporations in which they were interested, "with a resulting scarcity of stock when the news came out.

I knew that the new corporation which had recently taken over the old was supplied with an issue of common stock far in excess of what was to be used in the exchange for the old shares, and in this dividend announcement I read between the lines and was able to forecast much more accurately than if I had not been familiar with the past history of the Columbia, and had not studied du Pont methods of financing and development.

In the previous chapter you will find a reference to the technical position. It would be difficult to imagine one stronger than that prevailing in this stock after the news came out, because, in simple Wall Street parlance, "there was none of it for sale." And it was not long before the stock sold at over $300 per share.

During the summer, while I was on a long trip to Alaska and the Coast, I used to get the New York papers from seven to fifteen days late, but I knew that anything big or important would take several weeks to consummate, so I would have ample notice.

With frequent resting spells and reactions the stock climbed steadily to $400, and then to $500 per share, and with each fresh advance the stock dividends which were being distributed quarterly became more valuable; that is, the one-fifth of a share per annum (consisting of four quarterly payments of one-twentieth of a share) had a value of $40 per share when the stock sold at $200; $60 per share at $300; $80 per share at $400; and $100 per share when the price advanced to $500. It was the closest thing to "lifting itself by its boot-straps" that I had ever seen.

On the 40 shares the first dividend amounted to 2 shares; the second to 2.1 shares, making 44.1 shares. By that time the shadows of coming events began to show, for the company announced that it would shortly exchange the old stock of $100 par, for new stock of no par value, and that each holder of one share of old would receive ten shares of new stock. Occasional transactions on the Curb had been in the neighborhood of $500 per share, and now the new stock began to be traded in "when issued" between 43 and 50, and during the month of August, 1919, ran up as high as 59. At the low level of 431/2 to 46 during August and September the stock showed excellent resistance, while the rest of the market remained weak, and from its action I came to the conclusion that we were approaching the "fire-works" stage.

Along in October the stock was listed on the New York Stock Exchange and began to be very active, advancing rapidly several points per day until it reached 75. The volume of trading greatly increased. In some sessions there were from 50,000 to 75,000 shares dealt in, to say nothing of the odd lots which were not recorded. Numerous newspaper articles called attention to the company's development. I watched it work back and forth between 70 and 75, and when I saw certain indications appear, made up my mind that if it again declined to 70 I would sell part of what once was an odd lot.

The 44.1 shares were by that time exchanged for 441 shares of new stock, and soon afterward a dividend of a fraction over 22 shares

was received, making 463 shares, worth	$70
per share	$32,410.00
Plus three dividends at $2.50 per share on various lots..........	315.25
	$32,725.25
Less cost of original 40 shares and commissions.....................	6,575.00
Paper profit at $70 per share.......	$26,150.25

The stock dividends which were coming along quarterly amounted to 23 shares or $1,610 worth per quarter, or $6,440 per annum if the stock remained at $70. Add to this the cash dividends, which, on the new stock amounted to one-tenth of the old, and were being paid at the rate of 25 cents per share, or $1 per annum, the income amounted to about $6,900 on an original investment of less than $6,600.

That was a big percentage, provided the stock stayed at $70 per share, but the action of the stock indicated that insiders were selling at least a part of their line, perhaps enough to get back their original investment. Deciding that when insiders sell it is time for outsiders to sell, I disposed of 263 shares at 70, which gave back the original $6,575, besides $12,080.25 in cash, in addition to 200 shares paid for in full.

In fact, allowing for the profit and cash dividends, these 200 shares cost about $60 a share less than nothing. So I didn't see how my wife could lose on that transaction.

Selling part of the lot put me in a good position for another reason. If the insiders were to support the stock on a decline, then lift the price to a new high level, I could take advantage of it with the remainder of my holdings. But if, as was more likely, they allowed the stock to sag off, I could replace what I had sold at a lower level and then take advantage of any secondary advances and distribution that might occur.

The points to bear in mind in regard to this little deal in odd lots are these: I knew the industry, its present over-sold condition and its future trend. Also the position of the Columbia Company with relation thereto.

Inside information said the stock would advance 15 points. It was wrong; the price rose hundreds of points. The information on which I really acted was open to everyone. I confirmed the facts at the company's office.

By putting myself in the place of the insiders I was able to follow their reasoning and see the purpose behind their campaign. I took profits when they did, thus placing the account in a strong cash position, beyond the possibility of loss.

Surface or present conditions were not considered, but only the facts which indicated what the future would be. Technical conditions were closely watched for signs of moves by the insiders. Selling around the top provided the cash with which to replace at a lower figure. I did not get a full hundred per cent, of the possibilities in this little deal, but came mighty close to it.

My experience with American Graphophone shares show what can occasionally be done with odd lots, and disputes those who 'believe that fractional lots of stock are too small to bother with and should be ignored. I have described the matter in detail so that the reasons for every move are clearly set forth, and trust that the suggestions herein will be found of suggestive value to my readers.

JESSE L. LIVERMORE

Whose stock market operations are the most spectacular in the present generation.

VIII.
RULES I FOLLOW IN TRADING AND INVESTING

SOME people may form an impression, based on my previous articles, that when one acquires the proper amount of training and experience, making money by trading and investing in securities is an easy proposition. I hasten to correct either this impression or another which might also have been formed: that it is easy sailing for me personally.

I have yet to find the man, in or out of Wall Street, who is able to make money in securities, continuously or uninterruptedly. My experience is no different from that of many individuals who are known as successful Wall Street men. Like everyone else, I have my good and bad periods. Sometimes it appears as though everything I touch pans out well, and at other times everything seems to go wrong. It is much like any other line of business.

Success in trading means an excess of profits over losses. Success in the investment field means more good than bad investments. If anyone tells you he can be almost invariably successful, put him down as trying to impose on your credulity. One hundred per cent, accuracy was a height not even attained by the late J. P. Morgan. James R. Keene often said he was doing well if he could be right six times out of ten. I often used to call on him and watch him trading over his ticker on the fifth floor of the Johnson Building, 30 Broad Street, and there was many a time when I could plainly see from the nervous way in which he worked back and forth from his ticker to his telephone, and paced up and down the floor like a caged lion, that things were not going well. In his thirty or forty years. Wall Street career he went broke more than once.

I went into Harriman's office one day and found him a veritable bull in a china shop, because the market had been going contrary to his expectations.

In the present generation Jesse live more's operations are the most spectacular, but he is not by any means always right. Like all other traders, big or little, he makes serious mistakes at times. He has personally described to me his methods in detail. They provide for mistakes, accidents, errors in judgment and those unexpected happenings which every big or little operator must allow for.

One of the cleverest and most experienced traders on the floor of the New York Stock Exchange—a man who usually makes $300,000 a year out of his floor trading—said to me, "Whenever I take a position in a stock and find that it is running into a sufficient loss to amount to $20,000 or $25,000, and it begins to bother me in my day-to-day trading, I close it out."

Now go into the investment field and take the published annual list of investment securities owned by any of the big life insurance companies such as the Equitable, Mutual, New York Life or others who have the very best connections in the financial district, and whose investments are made under the advice and guidance of eminent financiers, attorneys, experts and actuaries. You find the same thing—frequent investments which turn out badly and which have to be written down and charged off.

Success in either field, therefore, depends upon whether your profits exceed your losses and income—how close you can come to one hundred per cent, accuracy. So no matter how long or how hard you study, nor how careful, conservative and experienced your guide, your counsel or your bankers, you must anticipate a certain portion of unfortunate investments and operations.

It is for this reason that many (but not all) of my investments are made with intent not only to realize large profits but to offset these occasional and unavoidable losses. I have found some men who claim that they never take a loss. This may be true, but I would rather take losses than take an inventory of the final result of such operations, because it is bound to show a number of securities that are miles away from their cost and which should be listed merely either as "Hopes" or "Faint Hopes."

This reminds me of a very clever trading rule followed by Jesse Livermore. Unless a stock shows him a profit within two or three days after he buys or sells it short, he closes the trade, on the ground that his judgment was wrong as to the immediate action of the stock, and he cannot afford to be tied up. He says, "Whenever I find myself *hoping* that a trade will come out all right, I get out of it."

Livermore's purpose in this rule is to keep his trading capital in circulation; never allowing it to become congested. It is a good rule. Think it over, and you will recall that you have often not only lost money by sticking to a hopeless proposition, but you have lost many, many opportunities.

Another Livermore principle is the cutting of losses. Of course, in his 10,000, 20,000 or 50,000 share campaigns he cannot place stop orders like a 100, 200 or 500 share trader, but he usually has a mental stop and when it is reached he closes out the trade.

It will be observed that Livermore, by the use of these two rules, has both a time and a price stop. He will not devote his margin (capital) to a transaction for more than a few days, and he will not let the trade run against him for more than a few points. While he, so far as I know, originated the first rule, the second, viz., the use of stop orders, has been one of the first principles of successful operators for many years. Harriman, Keene, and a host of others have advocated the absolute limitation of risk.

While I have made it a practice to limit my risk in most cases, I can trace most of my principal losses to my failure to place stop orders when the trades were made. And while I have always studied the limitation of risk and generally endeavored to trade in. a way that will keep the risk down to a minimum, I have very often delayed placing a stop order until the opportunity was lost, and in some cases these losses have run into five or ten points when they might just as well been limited to two or three. These incidents are of value because they show what should be avoided.

In trading I get the best results by watching carefully for an important turning point, limiting my risk, and trading for the ten or twenty point swings. But very often when I have the time to devote to it, and I feel myself in harmony with the market, I like to trade actively. Jumping in and out of stocks to the extent of 5,000 or 10,000 shares a day in the aggregate is a lot of fun , but is usually more profitable for the broker than for the trader, because of the immense handicap he is under in trying to pay commissions, taxes, and losses out of the small daily swings and get a profit besides. A trader on the floor of the New York Stock Exchange has an advantage over a non-member, whose total expenses on such business under the increased commission rates run from $1,000 to $2,000 a day.

The worth-while changes in security prices do not generally occur within the same session. The market movement or the situation which produces it must have time in which to develop. As Charles Hayden once said to me, ' * The day to buy is not the day to sell."

Subscribers to *The Magazine* frequently write me and explain that they are far removed from the market and ask whether they had not better come to New York or go to Chicago so as to be in "close touch with things." Very often this "closeness" is a handicap. One's real studying is done away from the market, not in a broker's office.

The best work I ever did in judging the market was when I devoted one hour a day in the middle of each session, I did not come to Wall Street. I had no news ticker. I seldom read the news items but judged solely from the action of the market itself; hence I was not influenced by any of the rumors, gossip, information or misinformation with which the Street is deluged day after day.

The out-of-town investor is therefore not under as much of a handicap as he might suppose. If he is trading and can get the result of the day's operation in time to give his orders next morning, he is better off than the majority of the people who come down here and hang over the ticker. His opinions are formed from the facts. He must know how to assemble these and draw the proper conclusions. But all he needs is the highest, lowest and last prices of the stocks which he is watching. Without being at all egotistical I believe I could go around the world and having arranged to have these few details of a stock like U. S. Steel or any other active issue cabled to me daily, I could cable my orders and come back with a profit. It would not be necessary for me to be advised of the volume of trading in, that stock or the general market, although in some instances this might help. Certainly I would not care to have any news of any kind included in the cables.

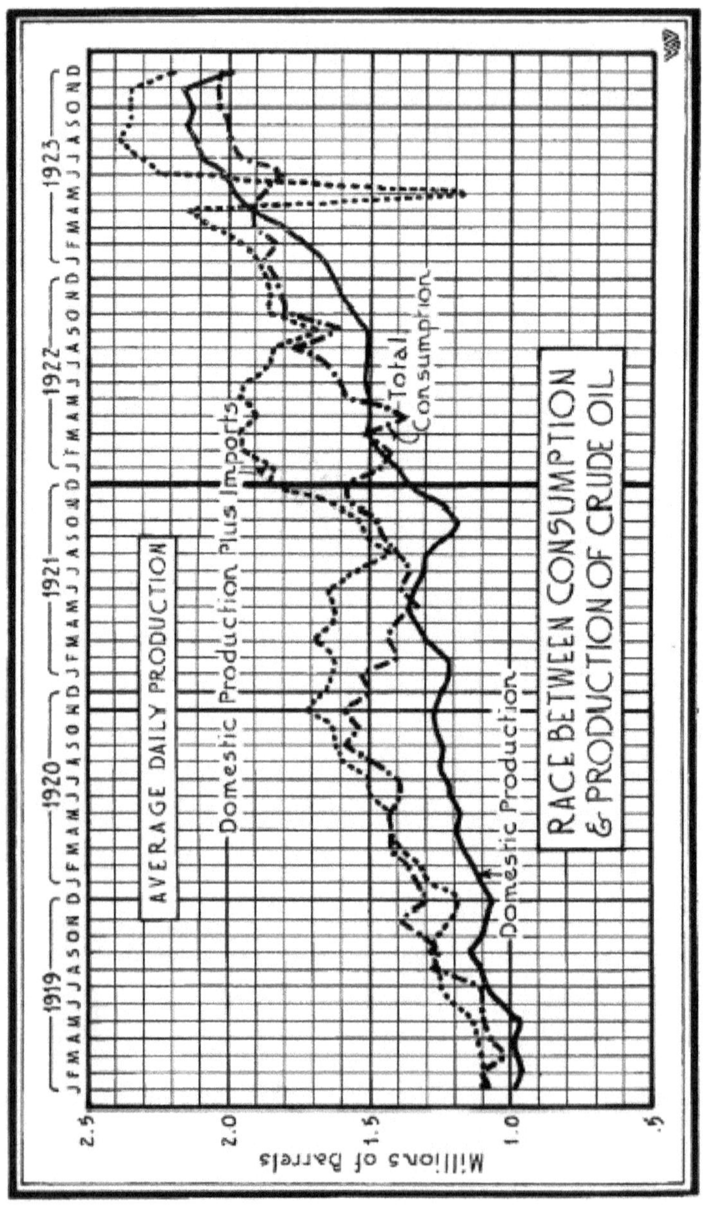

In the chapter which follows the fext refers only to the years 19 19-1921 shown in the above graph.

IX.
FORECASTING FUTURE DEVELOPMENTS

IN previous chapters I have referred to the value of foresight in the field of investment, and the advantages of keeping your money working where it will produce the best results in the shortest time, I like to go cross-lots toward an objective point. One way to do this is to keep a constant eye on the relative position of the different industries in order to see where the greatest advantage lies.

One hardly needs to do more than read the papers nowadays to form the opinion that certain industries are in an excellent position. But which of these is best?

The steel industry is apparently prosperous. The industry seems likely to go through in a belated way the filling of a vast commercial and industrial vacuum which resulted from the war's absorption of steel.

The resumption of building operations will be a big factor in the steel business for the next several years. We all know that the country is underbuilt, and a revival of building activity which has of late become apparent, means very big things for the steel trade.

Now that the railroads are back in the hands of their owners we may expect increased orders for rails, cars and locomotives, all of which will absorb quantities of steel. This should also produce a highly prosperous condition in the railway equipment business for some years to come.

I have been turning these matters over in my mind recently because I am very confident of the future of the market and I want to know which stocks in the most favored industry are likely to produce the most for me both from the standpoint of income and profit. Market movements, when correctly forecasted, pay more dollars than dividends.

While there are many of the minor industries in a very favorable position at present, I have concluded that one in particular stands head and shoulders above all the rest and that is the petroleum industry. The accompanying graph indicates that consumption has run ahead of production for the past two years and there is no sign of any change in this trend. This, in conjunction with the forecast by Walter C. Teagle, president of the Standard Oil Co. of N. J., gives us the backbone of the statistical position of oil. Mr. Teagle estimates that by 1925 the world will require 675,000,000 bbls. of crude oil against 376,000,000 produced in 1920 —an increase of 78 per cent. He asks where such an enormous quantity of oil is coming from. If he cannot tell, you and I need not guess.

Should any further assurance be required, we can refer to a report filed by the British Board of Trade in London whose Central Committee reported that demand was tending to outstrip the world's present supply.

It is plain, therefore, that there is a threatened world shortage of oil and that this situation cannot be cured for a long time to come. I am therefore putting money into the best class of oil stocks, for while there are many promising opportunities in other fields I regard this, for the time being, as the best industry in which to take a substantial position on the long side.

My reason is that the margin of profit in the producing and refining of oil, especially the former, will b6 a very substantial one—probably much larger, figuring on a per share basis, than in the steel, equipment, automobile, or other of the leading industries whose output may be expanded by the building of more plants and hiring more men. It is different with the oil business. Oil must be sought; and it is not always to be found where you expect to find it. Many of the old fields are playing out. Many of the 10,000 and 15,000 barrel gushers of a year ago are now running in the dozens or hundreds and in not a few cases have to be pumped at that.

The Ranger Field on July 1, 1919, was producing 160,000 bbls. a day. By February 1, 1920, this had dropped to 80,000 barrels daily. The Burkburnett Field has shown a very marked falling off, due to close drilling. Many of the biggest wells in Mexico have declined, owing to economic conditions, salt water invasion, or possible change of formation, due to volcanic eruptions.

There is a scarcity of new fields. We hear about discoveries in various sections of this and other countries, but it will require a good manyprolific fields to keep pace with the ravenous consumptive demand. It is apparent that in the oil industry there is no point of saturation, because the trade is continually working to make up a shortage which practically every year pulls down the visible supply.

The increase in the amount of machinery of all kinds and the elimination of hand labor is an important point in the demand, as each bit of machinery requires more lubrication and the lubricating material always has its base in crude oil. Automobiles are not only consumers of gasoline, but of great quantities of lubricating oil as well.

Tractors are developing another big new avenue of consumption and must in time supplant the horse on the farm, as the motor car has done in the cities. In Seattle there is not today a single horse, so far as I have been able to ascertain.

The year 1894 does not seem so long ago, yet when at that time I told some one that one of these days we would be traveling in horseless carriages, I was laughed at as being a dreamer.

Now I wish to record another similar dream.

It is that the streets of New York and all other great centers will, before many years, be underlaid with pipes which will carry fuel oil for use instead of coal in heating, manufacturing and other purposes. And here is a suggestion to any of my readers who are in a position to secure charters from their respective communities, for some day these charters will be worth a lot of money.

The day will soon pass when men shall be sent down into mines to haul up coal, put it on railroad trains, transport it hundreds of miles, unload it into coal carts, truck it through city streets, dump it into cellars and shovel it into furnaces.

Enormous oil tanks, similar to gas tanks now in use, should contain the liquid fuel which can be controlled by the mere turning of a valve or the operation of a thermostat.

No shovelling coal, or taking out ashes! This should make life in city or country more attractive, especially to those who have to hustle for the 5:15. But to the manufacturer, the owner of office buildings, or apartments, this development will have a much broader application, for it will mean the elimination of a number of factors that now contribute to the raising of rent, operating and manufacturing costs.

You may not follow this suggestion but somebody will, and a lot of somebodies will make a lot of millions in this way.

Practically every industry, from the peanut stand to the railroad locomotive and the enormous industrial plant, consumes oil in many ways. The world of machinery could not exist without oil. The use of machinery and particularly internal combustion motive power is spreading throughout the world. There are vast areas which are merely in the kerosene stage which will eventually be developed to the automobile and tractor stage. Carry the thought further and we see the likelihood that before many years we shall be shipping not only passengers but freight through the air, all of which means a still greater demand for crude oil to be converted into gasolene and lubricating oils.

These are some of the reasons why I have bought oil stocks during recent months. And why, in our Investment Letter, we have recommended these securities to our subscribers. By reason of the crying demand for crude, many of the refineries which have contracted to supply refined products are bidding against each other, so the companies which really hold the winning cards are the producers.

I anticipate a period of enormous profit-making in leading oil companies, particularly where they are intrenched in the field of production.

Most people make their mistake when averaging, by-starting too soon; or, if they are buying on a dose scale, say one point down, they do not provide sufficient capital to see them through in case the decline runs two or three times as many points as they anticipate. I recall a friend who, after seeing Union Pacific sell at 219 in August, 1909, thought it very cheap at 185 and much cheaper at 160. That made it a tremendous bargain at 135. He bought at all those figures. But at fi6, his capital was exhausted, and, as they put it in Wall Street, "he went out with the tide."

X.
TRUTH ABOUT "AVERAGING DOWN"

A GREAT deal of money is lost or tied up by people who make a practice of averaging. Their theory is that if they buy a security at 100 and it goes to 90, it is that much cheaper, and the lower it goes the cheaper it grows. Like all Wall Street rules and theories, this is sometimes true; but there are a great many times when a security will decline in market price while its intrinsic value and earning power are shrinking even more swiftly.

While a decline in price is often due to a slump in the general market for bonds or stocks, or both, owing to some circumstance affecting a certain group of stocks, it also frequently occurs that the price is going down because of an inherent weakness in the company's affairs or a diminution of its prospects. knowledge of such an influence is often confined to the few who are in close touch with the company's affairs. Sometimes there is a gradual development toward the unfavorable side; then again there may be an overnight happening which causes a radical change in former estimates or value.

Whatever the cause of a decline, the question of averaging is one that puzzles people who have bought at higher prices and are wondering whether averaging is not a good way out. Very often it proves to be the way to get in deeper. Hence, in order intelligently to judge whether to average, it is necessary to know what caused the decline.

I remember, a few years ago, buying a certain stock at around 45. Sometime after I bought it the price declined to about 30, at which point I afterward learned the stock was underwritten; so that to the insiders everything above 30 represented profit.

The company was doing a splendid business but the stock had been badly handled, and those who were responsible for its market action ran away and left the new baby on the public's door-step. Knowing that the stock was in the hands of the public, I did not average at 30, but waited until it was down to around 15. Then

I bought an equal amount. This I sold at ten points profit which marked my original cost down to $35. The stock then declined to 12 and I bought again, re-selling at 16, reducing my cost to about 31. Some months later it advanced to 38, where I sold. This let me out about even, allowing for interest.

These transactions ran over two or three years and serve to illustrate a good way of averaging out on a bond or stock which has been disappointing in its action. It is a method employed by large interests who, as previously described, often work on a much closer scale and take advantage of all the small variations in the market.

Why did I buy the stock when it was down? And why didn't I sell at a loss? Because I made investigations through the company's officials, and found that the corporation was in a very prosperous condition, having reduced its obligations and increased its earning power during the time when the stock was declining from 45 to a fraction of that figure. It was a case where intrinsic values were on the increase while the market price was decreasing.

Thus I kept myself always in a position where I could buy more in case it went still lower and by selling on the rallies I provided the funds for repurchasing. Having bought the first lot (to average around 15) I was then in a position to sell it on a rally and re-buy it on a decline, so that whichever way the market went I would benefit. Had the price declined to 10 and then 5, 1 would probably have bought an equal amount or perhaps double the quantity at the low level—always with my eye on the compass, which was the company's physical, financial and commercial condition.

Stocks like this sometimes decline of their own technical weight, that is, the amount of shares that are pressing in liquidation, combined with an absence of support; or they may be put down—that is, artificially depressed by those who are desirous of accumulating at the low levels. In this case I believe there was a combination of both influences.

Most people make their mistake when averaging, by starting too soon; or, if they are buying on a close scale, say one point down, they do not provide sufficient capital to see them through in case the decline runs two or three times as many points as they anticipate.

I recall a friend who, after seeing Union Pacific sell at 219 in August, 1909, thought it very cheap at 185 and much cheaper at 160. That made it a tremendous bargain at 135. He bought at all those figures. But at 116, his capital was exhausted and, as they put it in Wall Street, "He went out with the tide."

Eighty-five or ninety per cent, of the business, investment and speculative mortalities are due either to over-trading or lack of capital, which when boiled down are one and the same thing. And those who average their investment or speculative purchases supply in a great many instances, glaring examples of the causes of failure.

Years ago, when Weber & Fields formed one of the star theatrical attractions in New York, they used to have a scene in a bank where one of the team was the banker and the other the customer of the institution.

The "official" observing his "customer" at the wicket, made the very pertinent inquiry, "Put in or take out?"

I was reminded of this recently when thinking of the number of people who come down to the Street year after year, and with varying results (mostly bad, I must agree), keep on putting in and taking out until they either make a success or a failure of it. And I am continually asking myself, as a sort of test question, whether in putting in or taking out I am making progress or going backward. Like the frog who was trying to jump out of the well, I sometimes slip, but every year I can see that I am making progress.

There are seasons when it pays me to stick very close to shore, because, by reason of other influences, my judgment is not up to par. Sometimes, however, I am stubborn enough to keep on fighting through these periods, because no one can stay in the security market for a great many years without growing used to punishment. It has already been explained that success means more good than bad investments or ventures, so the readers of previous chapters will understand just what I mean.

Everyone should occasionally sit down and take account of stock—not securities, but his own ability, judgment, and what is most important, results thus far obtained. If he finds that the past few months or years have been unsatisfactory and unprofitable, judging from the amount of time, thought, study, and capital employed, he should suspend operations until he ascertains the cause; then he should set about to cure it. This can be done by study and practice (on paper or with ten share lots or single thousand dollar bonds if necessary) until he is confident that he has overcome the difficulty.

It may be that he is a chronic bull and finds himself in a bear market. I have frequently discovered that I was out of tune with the market, although I am never a chronic bull or bear, but always the kind of an animal the situation seems to call for.

It has been a great advantage to me, however, to have gone off by myself at times and figured out just where I stood, and, if things were going wrong, why? I find that it is more important to study my misfortunes than my triumphs.

JAMES R. KEENE

Who advised the "absolute limitation of risk" in market operations. Keene was one of the shrewdest traders Wall Street ever knew.

XI. CONCLUSIONS AS TO FORESIGHT AND JUDGMENT

IT must be apparent from the foregoing chapters, that during the years I have spent in Wall Street I have not only kept my eyes and ears open, but have gained much as a result of study, practice and experience. It is logical to suppose that I have formed certain definite conclusions with regard to the business of trading and investing, and that these, if frankly and clearly stated and fully appreciated by those who read, should be of considerable value to the many who have not devoted so much time or effort in the same line of work.

No one can stay at it for even a short time without acquiring a certain knowledge, And it is for each to decide whether he is content to plod along in a desultory way, or go in for an intensive study of the subject. My recommendation to readers is that they take it up seriously even if they have not a single dollar to invest at present. The time will come when they will have funds for investment and the greater their store of information on the subject, the greater the incentive for saving or acquiring money in any legitimate way and the more profitable the outcome.

In an atmosphere of deceptive surface indications and false news, reports, gossip, methods, etc., such as one encounters in Wall Street, it is sometimes difficult to know just what one is trying to do and how well or how badly he is doing it. It is not easy to size yourself up and to see just what are your basic principles, and how well you are following them.

Whenever a situation is not entirely clear to me, I find I can clarify it by putting down on paper all the facts, classifying them as favorable and unfavorable. In thus writing it out on paper I not only have time to reason out each point as I go along, but when I get it all down it can be looked over and analyzed to much better advantage.

Following this idea I have written down perhaps fifty different conclusions which I have reached with regard to the business of trading and investing, and these I will take up, one after the other in this and later chapters, for they constitute a partial list of principles which should be recognized and applied, according to individual requirements.

These points are about equally divided between investment and speculation, but it is so difficult to determine where one begins and the other ends that in many cases I shall be obliged to treat them in combination. The thing we are trying to accomplish is an increase in our personal wealth, and whether this is done by the careful investment and slow accretion of money, the income of which is reinvested in order to enhance the principal sum, or whether we endeavor to increase our principal by attempting to forecast movements of security prices and to profit thereby—all that is something which each person must decide for himself.

Both My Primary and My Ultimate Object Is the Safe and Profitable Investment op My Funds.

I say primary because that is my first and principal object and I use the term ultimate because eventually I expect to become an investor for income only. Provision for himself and family during the later years of his life is what every red-blooded man is working for. Some men—James R. Keene was one—continue to trade in stocks until they are very old. But most people want to feel that from at least sixty on they will be free from the necessity of making money on which to live during their declining years.

Trading profits should therefore be used to increase the principal sum which is invested in income-bearing securities, preferably those which will grow in market value. Income from such investments should be made to compound itself by re-investing it as received.

If One is Not Adapted to Trading He Should Prove it to His Own Satisfaction and Then Abandon the Business.— He should then attempt to become an intelligent and successful investor. Failing of this, he should turn to savings banks and mortgages or other non-fluctuating mediums for the investment of his funds.

A friend of mine once had something over $100,000 worth of bonds, a few of which he deposited with a broker as margin. The bonds were his backlog; they represented the result of his savings from the time he first entered business, and were bringing in a good income, besides having possibilities. As he traded back and forth, he found that he was gradually taking some of the bonds which he had in his box, and putting them up with the broker, until finally he reached a point where nearly half of the bonds were gone. This, he decided, was conclusive evidence of the fact that he was not adapted to the business of trading. He therefore discontinued trading and resumed the saving tactics by which he had accumulated the first hundred bonds.

That was some years ago. He has now over $200,000 worth, and when at rare intervals he ventures into the speculative arena, he does it very timidly and with only trifling sums.

I recommend this man's course to those who have had similar experiences, but with this exception: If they are willing to devote themselves to the task, they will doubtless overcome their difficulties and be more successful with the added study and experience. But to go right on putting good money after bad, not only reflects on a man's business judgment but indicates a weakness in his character which he had best conquer in short order.

The experiences of our earlier years are well and cheaply bought if we really profit by them.

No one can avoid having his capital tied up at times in mediums which are not satisfactory. But there should be no hesitation about switching, even though it necessitates the taking of a loss in your present holdings. A good security will make up this loss much faster than one which is mediocre. So the question which one should ask himself with relation to all of the securities which he holds, is this: "Are there any other issues which will work for me more profitably and in a shorter time than these? I cannot afford to let money sleep, nor have it work slowly. I am like a merchant: I must turn my money over as often as I can, so that the average yearly return will be at its maximum."

One's Capital Should Be Made to Do the Greatest Service in the Shortest Length of Time.—This applies both to trading capital and investment capital. I have found that it is best to use only a small part of the total available capital for trading. To employ all or most of it is a fatal mistake, for in case of an unforeseen situation, causing a large loss, one is obliged to begin over again; whereas if the bulk of the capital is invested where it is safe, returns an income, and will probably enhance in value, then in case of a calamity a part of it can be turned into cash in order to renew trading operations.

But this should occur in only rare instances. When a man finds that he has a certain sum invested and that this sum is diminishing on account of his pulling it down for trading purposes, he is on the wrong track and had better stop short and take account of himself before he travels further. A person who cannot be successful in trading with a small amount of capital, will unquestionably lose a large amount if he employs it.

In making one's capital do the greatest amount of work in the shortest length of time, it is necessary to be forever on the lookout for better opportunities than those which you now have. If you hold bonds which are selling between 90 and 95, and which may, in a good bond market, advance to 110, you would not be justified in retaining them if you can buy another bond which is just as well secured, just as marketable, and has all the other good points of your present security, besides being convertible into a security which has excellent prospects of an advance to a very much higher figure.

Should you own a preferred stock which is paying its 7 per cent, and showing on the average only one and a half times its dividends, whereas you can buy, at the same price, another preferred stock which is earning three or four times its dividend, taking the average of a number of years, it is by all means best to make the exchange. It is highly important to find out just what we can and cannot do, but we should not be discouraged too soon. I have met thousands y and thousands of people who were endeavoring to make money in speculation and regret to say that very few are really qualified to become successful traders of any importance.

But there are hundreds of thousands of successful investors, and it is toward this avenue of success and independence that I hope to turn the attention of most of my readers. By studying "the public" and its ways, I have learned what kind of operations the majority are best fitted for; while it is a peculiar fact that very few people delude themselves into thinking that they are good physicians, surgeons, lawyers or dentists, they do try to fool themselves into believing that they are good investors and speculators.

Look around you—do you find that among your acquaintances 100% are well-to-do and successful business men? Are not the majority just plodding along, neither getting rich nor poor? Well, that is just as true in Wall Street as it is in business. You can generally pick the brilliant successes and count them on the fingers of one or both hands, depending on the size of your circle of acquaintances.

People are successful in business because, while they make mistakes at first, they study these mistakes and avoid them in future. Then by gradually acquiring a knowledge of the basic principles of success, they develop into good business men. But how many apply this rule to their investing and trading? Very few do any studying at all. Very few take the subject seriously. They drift into the security market, very often "get nipped," as the saying is, avoid it for a while, return from time to time with similar results, then gradually drift away from it, without ever having given themselves a chance to develop into what might be good traders or intelligent investors.

This is all wrong. People go seriously into the study of medicine, the law, dentistry, or they take up with strong purpose the business of manufacturing of merchandising, but very few ever go deeply into this vital subject which should be seriously undertaken by all.

Now we all admit that the average man is mentally lazy. He hates work, mental or physical, doesn't want to spend an hour every evening, or even once a week, except at bridge, poker, or something else equally diverting and interesting. Those who do employ their time profitably are headed toward wealth and independence; but in many cases the poker players will later be supported by their children.

But to return to our subject, it should not take more than a few years for a person to find out whether he is qualified for trading or whether he should devote himself to the investment side of the proposition.

THE CULTIVATION OF FORESIGHT IS MOST ES-SENTIAL.—In the main it is the man with the greatest amount of foresight who is most successful in the security market. Foresight is the very essence of speculation. Without the use of it a person is not speculating at all— he is merely taking chances—gambling.

One of the late J. P. Morgan's strong points was his ability to foresee and therefore to anticipate the vast changes in financial conditions and security prices. It was marvelous how he frequently predicted, months in advance, the outcome of certain involved business and financial situations which were not understood or anticipated by anyone else. This was one of the qualities that made him great. It enabled him to engage in vast undertakings, of which the U. S. Steel Corporation is a conspicuous example, but there are many other industrial monuments to his financial genius which was, after all, built around his marvelous foresight. It was foresight which made E. H. Harriman a great man. It enabled him to anticipate the development of the Union Pacific and Southern Pacific Railroads and nerved him to undertake the stupendous task of creating a railroad empire.

Harriman once held an ordinary job—just like you and I once did, or do now—and if he, through the cultivation of foresight, and the other qualities which made him pre-eminent, could accomplish such splendid results, then you and I can, by the exercise of the talents with which we are blessed, advance our personal fortunes by concentrating on the development of our own foresight. It will prove of value, not only in our investments, but in every undertaking which we enter—financial, business or personal—during our whole lives. So let us give close attention to the subject. A large part of such success as I have already attained is due to my having formed the habit of looking ahead to see in what direction future events are likely to run.

It Is Better to Depend on Your Own Judgment Than on That of Any Other Person.— If you have not reached a point where you can do this, better continue your studies and practice until you can form a sound, independent judgment on which you can base your commitments.

"We hear a great deal in Wall Street about "inside information" and the value of big connections. But I have found that the man who depends the most on his own judgment is headed for success if he has not already attained it. It is very easy to be swayed by the multitudinous opinions that are bandied around the Street and which may be had for nothing because they are generally worth it.

Suppose you are a most intimate personal friend of a man who is putting through a big deal in a security which is listed on the New York Stock Exchange. He tells you all the facts and puts you in a position to buy, with a thorough knowledge of what is going on. You do buy, and perhaps you make money, but more often than not it will turn out when you come to realize, you will be so enthused by your inside knowledge that you will not sell at the right time, or a hitch will occur which turns your profit into a loss, or your big man is out of town, or something is happening to the market which he cannot explain.

But suppose you do get away with a profit— you are apt to be so carried off your feet that at your very next opportunity you will think you have Wall Street by the tail and will plunge with all you have made and all you have besides, and eventually end up with a loss. The kind of money which does you the most good is that which you make through your own efforts. All "Wall Street is trying to get something for nothing. Don't join the crowd. Rather, "buck it"—the crowd is generally wrong. Become one of the successful few who build stone upon stone until they have a solid foundation of knowledge and experience which will last them all their lives.

If I believed that the people who are now reading and studying the numerous articles which appear in The Magazine would, five or ten years from now, still be looking to it for easy ways to make money, I should be very much discouraged. But if, as I believe, a great many will, through its teachings, be induced to become students and ultimately intelligent and successful investors, then I will feel that the many years of hard work which I have put into the publication have been well rewarded.

Down in New Street, on the block between Wall Street and Exchange Place, you will find, on any pleasant day, a lot of Wall Street "Ghosts" sunning themselves. And by way of explanation let me say that a Wall Street Ghost is one who has tried to make money in the market and failed. He is the saddest sight in all the financial district. Once a prosperous and perhaps wealthy business man, he is now reduced to mere driftwood among the eddies which surround the Stock Exchange. In and out of the brokerage offices you find him rambling in a hopeless fashion, always on the lookout for "tips." The red-headed bootblack and Jim, the shoe-lace man, are types of his confidants. He always know where everything is going, but never gets anywhere himself.

I don't know what becomes of these old "Ghosts" who drift about the old stamping ground, but it is instructive to know that their ranks are recruited from the people who never tried to cultivate a judgment of their own, but always depended on that of others.

THE LONGER YOUR EXPERIENCE THE BETTER BACKGROUND YOU HAVE FOR COMPARISON, AND THE GREATER YOUR ABILITY TO JUDGE AND FORE-CAST CORRECTLY—As Conditions are constantly changing, no two markets are alike and no two daily sessions are similar; but markets and sessions and panics and booms all have certain characteristics which should be carefully studied and intimately understood.

The man who has never been through a panic would be apt to find himself badly rattled. Under a pressure of excitement and nervous strain he would probably do the wrong thing. But anyone who has experienced a number of panics, knows how to conduct his operations so as to take the utmost advantage of such a rare opportunity, provided he has previously put himself in a position to buy at the low prices.

To some people it may be discouraging to say that you must keep at this business for many years in order to become highly successful; but is not this what you must do in your own line of business? Are not the best business and professional men those who have had the longest practice?

You cannot go into any phase of endeavor and make money or become prominent "just like that"—you must serve your apprenticeship. Of course, if you want to join the ranks of the large percentage of people who spend their declining years in the care or custody of their children or relatives, or in institutions, then you can afford to ignore my suggestion that work and study and long experience are essential. But if you have imagination and can picture yourself as possessing wealth and contentment in your old age, you will immediately admit that it is well worth your while to devote serious attention to this subject.

You have to live anyhow, so why not live well? It all depends on you, for you can generally take out in as great a measure as you put in.

By long experience I do not mean merely reading the financial columns for thirty or forty years; one does not gain experience in that way. I refer to the practical experience of investing in stocks and bonds; making mistakes; finding out why and profiting thereby in future.

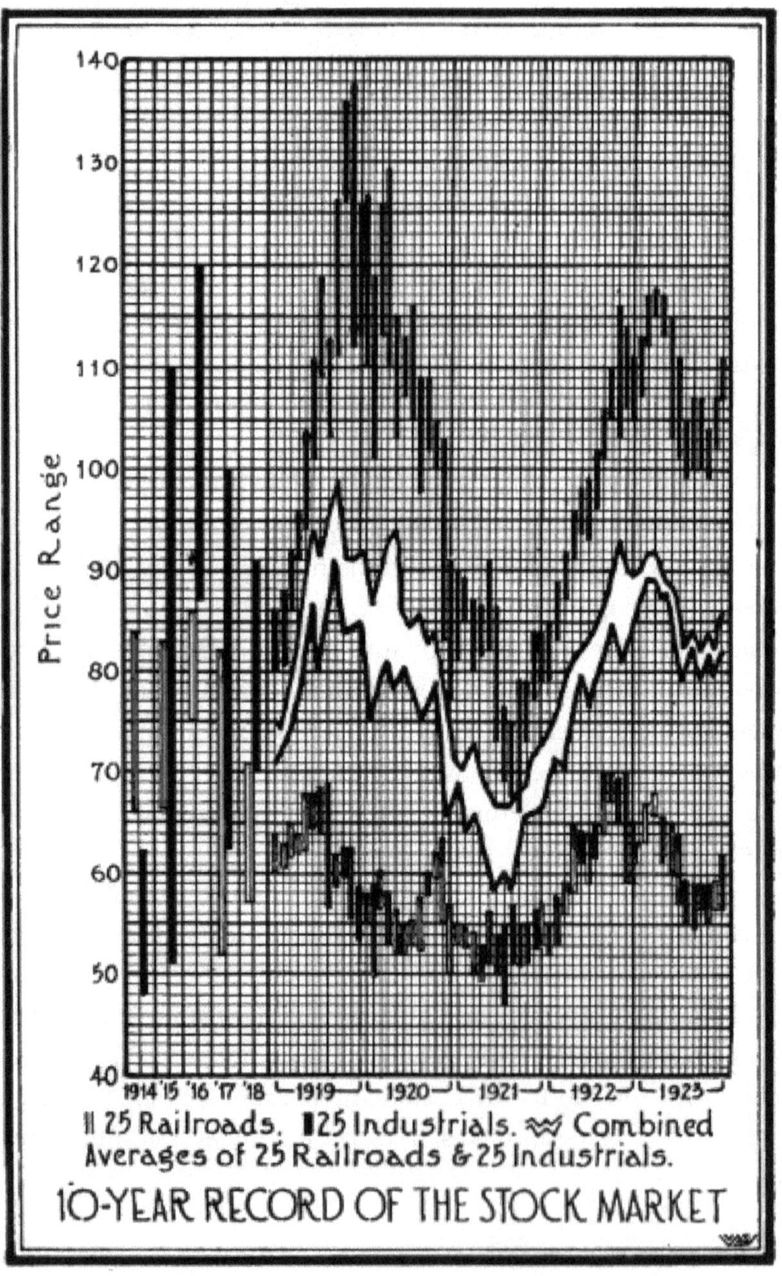

10-YEAR RECORD OF THE STOCK MARKET

XII. SAFEGUARDING YOUR CAPITAL

THE question is not whether you can make money with your original capital but whether you will cease because of the loss of this initial money at the very outset.

There is everything in getting a good start. In a preceding chapter it was shown that I did not begin to invest until eight years after my studies had commenced, and that I did not begin trading until six years after that. Just how long the average investor should pursue his studies without putting his ideas into practical operation is a matter for each individual to decide, but there should be a thorough understanding of the theoretical side before the first ventures or investments are actually made.

A person becomes competent in other fields because he has generally gone through a long period of practice and preparation. A physician for example, goes to college, attends clinics, rides in an ambulance, serves in hospitals, and, after some years of preparatory work, hangs out a sign. In Wall Street the same M.D. would hang out his sign first; then proceed to practice. In one way the doctor's work, in and out of Wall Street, bears resemblance, inasmuch as when he begins to practice "his profession he has to acquire patients. In Wall Street it is spelled "patience." Both are absolutely necessary to his success.

The Magazine of Wall Street has often repeated Warnings against beginning to operate before you know how; but the truth will bear many repetitious, and at our circle of readers is constantly widening we are again emphasizing this point.

If Wall Street could only retain the same clientele year after year and add to it the many who for the first time find themselves with investment or trading capital, we should have four million and five million share days instead of one and two million. It is strange that in the financial district, which is the very heart of the nation's commercial and industrial structure, there is such a woeful lack of understanding of what the public requires in the way of assistance.

My organization has devoted a great deal of effort to showing the brokerage houses that in order to permanently retain their clients, steps should be taken to educate them. We have offered to sell the banking, brokerage and investment houses quantities of literature at cost and have tried to show the brokerage fraternity how important it is to disseminate educational books and pamphlets on this subject, in order that their clients, through genuine knowledge, might become permanent instead of transient, patrons of their respective houses. But with rare exceptions, our appeals have fallen upon ears that were deaf. Brokers would rather go on securing^ at great expense, new clients to take the place of those who become discouraged and fall by the wayside. Someday a brokerage house will be evolved which has, as a permanent part of its organization, an educational department whose business it will be to see that its clients are properly informed as to just what they should do and how they should do it. Meantime, the individual investor is deprived of assistance from the logical source whence it should come.

The people who really stay at the business and continue year after year to buy and sell securities can generally be classified into two divisions. First, those who have outside sources of income and are continually bringing money into the street, and, second, those who are successful in their operations and thereby increase their capital, or to a greater or lesser extent maintain themselves out of what they thus realize. It is unfortunate that the percentage of those who bring money to Wall Street is so large and that many do not realize that it is their lack of knowledge and their inefficient methods in the financial field which bring such unsatisfactory results.

Lawyers, doctors, surgeons and other professional men are obliged, under state laws, to pass certain examinations and receive certifiicates showing that they are competent to practice. This is for the protection of the public, but no way has been provided whereby the public can be protected against its own operations in the security market. It would be a good thing if the financial lives of more customers of brokerage houses could be sustained by making them pass an examination as to knowledge of the subject and ability to take care of themselves. Many states require applicants to pass an examination before they are given permission to drive an automobile on the public highways. In one ease it is a physical and in the other a financial risk.

A certain amount of mistakes and a percentage of unfortunate investments are to be expected, no matter how well you start or how expert you become. But you should always preserve your trading or investment capital by never putting yourself in a position to have this wiped out. As the Irishman said, "It is betther to be hurted than kilt." Lack of capital and over-trading, being the cause of most misfortunes, are the result of being too heavily committed in one direction or another.

Investors who begin with even a single one hundred dollar capital have the choice of being conservative or of over-trading, but through ignorance many do not realize just when they are over-reaching and when their operations may be designated as conservative. In order to avoid a danger, they must know where it lies. It would be foolish for a corporal to lead an army into a strange country; and just as foolish for any novice to marshal his capital and launch into one or another phase of buying or selling stocks or bonds, without previous study.

A cross-section of the public's operations would show lack of interest when prices are low and the market is dragging along. When prices begin to advance the public begins to buy and this buying increases in proportion to the extent and rapidity of the advance until, at the top of an important movement, the public is 95% bullish and, as a rule, loaded up. The more uninterrupted the advance, the greater and more rapid the increase in public commitments.

Examining the cross-section in a panic we would find that those who went heavily long on the way up and at the top are selling out or being sold out. The buying is by new recruits, consisting of bargain-hunting people who have never before bought securities, combined with the comparatively few who sold while prices were high, and who therefore have money to invest.

Prices may have advanced steadily for a couple of years prior to the panic and those who began with a small amount of capital may have accumulated good round sums when figured at the high prices—mostly paper profits. But as bear markets are generally both swift and severe, these profits are quickly swept away, so that often those who have been piling them up for two years often lose them in thirty or sixty days.

You may say to yourself: "Oh, well, the public may do that, but I'm not one of the public." But the fact is unless you are a trained and experienced trader or investor, or have, to some extent, a claim to being an insider, a professional or semi-professional, then you are one of that vast majority which constitutes the great American speculative and investing public. The sooner you realize this fact the more quickly you can adjust yourself to your proper position in the financial scale.

The point of difference between the public and those who are not of this class is found in the fact that the public is not sophisticated; in other words, not trained in the business. If you are trained, you are not a member of that body.

Having thus classified yourself it is your business to ascertain how you can proceed without danger to the point where you can safely and profitably depend upon your own judgment. My personal opinion is that this can best be done by a course of study before beginning operations, because a satisfactory outcome is the result of knowledge plus capital. If you lack either the knowledge or the capital or both you cannot succeed, so the logical course is to get the knowledge first, meanwhile saving or setting aside the capital.

It is stupidity which makes people "rush in where angels fear to tread." And there is something about the Wall Street atmosphere which makes people think that whatever is to be done must be done at once, otherwise the opportunity will get away from them. I find that opportunities are coming along all the time, and that the majority are not as good as they look. So the best ones are worth waiting for.

The young man with his first money might very well spend his spare time for five years in study, investigation, self-training, in order to find out whether he is an investor, a trader, or a speculator, and the more he learns about it the greater he will realize how very ignorant he was at the beginning. If, at the age of thirty, he sees the necessity for study, and at thirty-five he has accumulated some capital which in the meantime has been reposing in the savings banks or in high grade bonds or mortgages, he should not even then go in with the idea of cleaning up a fortune, but with intent to cautiously and conservatively proceed, so that during the entire balance of his life he will steadily build up his fund of investment knowledge and capital on a constantly broadening base.

This matter is not anything that has to be hustled—you can pursue your regular business with this as a side line or hobby, if you like. You can't learn everything in a minute, but of course the more time you can devote to it the more rapidly you can proceed to practice.

The main point, as I have said, is to so preserve your initial capital that you will never be deprived of it, and the way to do this is to learn what you are about before you go about it.

It is well to study the methods of other large and successful operators and investors.

Much can be learned from this source. There is great value in imitation, but of course we must select the individuals whose methods have been scientific and whose results speak for themselves.

When I was a small boy I became interested in the study of music. Some of my teachers were better qualified than others, but the one under whom I made the most progress was the one who interested me in the broad aspect of the art by inducing me not merely to practice hard but to attend the best of concerts and operas; to study the theory of music, the history of great composers, the characteristics of great compositions, the principles of harmony, etc. This teacher would, when I was learning a particularly difficult passage on the piano or organ, sit down and play it for me so that I could imitate. The result was that I became so interested in my lessons that I devoted to them practically all of my spare time and money.

That is the way to go into this subject. While you cannot expect big financiers or large and successful traders to sit down and tell you just how they do it, there is, in these enlightened days, a world of literature bearing on the subject. Past volumes of *The Magazine* contain many articles of this nature. Your public libraries are all supplied with helpful material. Many hints are to be derived from a study of the methods of successful men.

> There is no place in the modern world for the unskilled; no one can hope for any genuine success who fails to give himself the most complete special education. Good intentions go for nothing, and industry is thrown away if one cannot infuse a high degree of skill into his work. The trained man has all the advantages on his side; the untrained man invites all the tragic possibilities of failure."

XIII. HOW MILLIONS ARE LOST IN WALL STREET

MANY years ago there was a stock dealt in on the New York Curb called Arlington Copper. The "mine" was said to be over a hundred years old and, with the modern methods which could be applied to the low-grade ore in the property, the promoters claimed they would be able to make a very big profit.

The seat of this operation was at Arlington, N. J., a small residential town just across the meadows from Jersey City. One could step on an Erie train and be there in twenty minutes. He could have seen a lot of old workings, and a lot of rock that was pointed out as ore. The round trip might have cost a dollar and occupied three hours.

Did any of the people who eagerly purchased the stock on the Curb take a trip over to Arlington to see what they were buying? They did not. They were "too busy," or they had to be home at 6:30, as they had a "dinner engagement." Possibly their meal time or their evening's social affair was more important than the many thousands of dollars which they put into this stock, but in any event Arlington Copper passed away as many "good things" are apt to do.

One does not have to look far to find many illustrations of this point. The public does not investigate, but buys and sells on somebody's say-so, and without using the precautions that would surely be applied in its own particular line of business.

For many years I have been impressed with the necessity of having investigation precede investments, instead of succeeding them. Take the field of patents and calculate, if you can, how many hundreds of millions are sunk each year in somebody's new-fangled idea as to how this or that should be done. In discussing this matter with an expert mechanical engineer the other day, it developed that 97% of the patents that are taken out are either of no commercial value or are never developed to a point where they realize a profit. Yet, as he said, "There are many big men in this town whose ear you can get quicker with a new patented appliance than in any other way. They will lay aside their own line of business and take up your new mechanism, if it is something that tickles their fancy." But that is only one field.

It is impossible to estimate how many hundreds of millions are lost because of improper preliminary investigation of the commercial, financial and technical aspects of the enterprises which absorb such a large proportion of the public wealth. Yet there is no other way in which money may be so intelligently spent as in safeguarding capital.

Most people do not know how to investigate an enterprise. Someone comes along with a newly patented washing machine. He needs $25,000 to "develop it." He would like to get you and some of your friends to put up $5,000 each. He will give you 51% interest in the business. He invites investigation. But you and your friends do not really investigate—you get hold of somebody who is already in the washing machine business and ask what he thinks of it. He is not an expert; he doesn't know the patent situation—all he knows is whether he can sell the machine he is now handling and whether he thinks this is better than his, but he has no broad understanding of the business because all he is. handling is one little machine in one little comer of the U.S.A. A few hundred or a few thousand dollars spent in a thorough investigation would save a lot of trouble, time and money.

The same principle applies to an oil, mining, railroad, industrial, or any other kind of enterprise. Money spent in careful investigation is insurance against loss. It is also productive of information which will be valuable in case you desire to go into the business or buy shares.

An enterprise in which I have an interest has recently decided to put a new product on the market. The demand had been established and greatly exceeded the supply. There was no question as to the company's ability to make the goods and sell them, but there was a question as to just what grade of goods would best please the public and just how they should be sold. So a very broad survey of the whole industry was ordered, with the result that the company is now in a position to go forward with its new goods in an intelligent way, along the line of least resistance. It is this sort of pre-vision which makes for success.

It is a remarkable and confirmatory fact that the officials of this company frequently take speculative fliers and make investments in securities, but their investigations seldom go beyond the stage of a surface inquiry as to the opinion of one or two parties, including the broker who is at the other end of the telephone listening for an order.

That reminds me of a point I have often made as to the ethics involved, in the client asking and the broker giving an opinion as to a contemplated investment or speculation. Personally, I believe that the client should know what he wants to do before he approaches the broker and that the latter 's function is to execute the order and finance the operation. Many people do not agree with me, but it is a matter which we may take up for discussion at another time.

Perhaps you cannot investigate personally, owing to lack of time or knowledge of the subject, but you can always secure the services of those who can. In one of my previous chapters I stated some of my experiences in mining stocks and showed how I employed mining engineers to examine properties and other engineers to check them up. Mining is only one form of industry which is represented in Wall Street, and I should say that there are many, many more enterprises besides mines that need investigation. Within the past several months a number of propositions have been shown up as representing but a fraction of the value originally claimed for them by the promoters.

What Wall Street needs is some means of "checking up" on the enthusiasm and, in some cases, the deception of those who are engaged in marketing securities. There are two kinds of people in the financial district: those who are trying to help themselves by helping others, and those who are helping themselves to what others possess. It does not take long to find out whether those with whom you are dealing belong to the preferred class.

Investigation of some of the enterprises whose securities are dealt in, is a subject calling for a Very wide range of knowledge and ability, and is beyond the reach of the average man. An examination of a property like the Philadelphia Company, for example, or Cities Service or Ohio Cities Gas would require training in a great many different fields, many of which the average investor does not understand. A thorough investigation of such an enterprise would only be justified by a very large investment.

It is for this reason that such a large percentage of people who buy securities are stockholders in U. S. Steel, because the steel business is something they understand, or think they do, and the Steel Corporation is a leader in the frequency and detail of its periodical reports, containing essential statistics of which almost anybody can understand the main features. If some other corporations with complex organizations would make their operations so well understood to the average investor, and by past performances attain such a degree of confidence in the minds of the public, many people might sell their U. S. Steel and buy the other securities. But with the Steel Corporation occupying a position, of prominence similar to a mountain surrounded by little hills, it is easy for anyone to see just where the mountain stands and its relative breadth and height compared with its neighbor's.

The more I study this subject, the greater appears the necessity for "investigation before investing." In the matter of discrimination alone there is such a wide range of conditions and so many angles from which comparisons may be made, that the subject is, except in some instances, highly complicated and calls for a clear and expert judgment before deciding upon a definite course.

Next in importance to knowing what to buy is the question as to when it should be done.

I was discussing this matter with an investor today. He referred to the assets and earning power of a big corporation whose securities had recently suffered a very material decline. He could not understand why the stock should go down in the face of such a showing of commercial and financial strength.

My answer was this: ' 'You have an automobile—it consists of a lot of steel, wood, rubber, brass, leather and other material. It requires gasoline, water, air and lubricating oil. Also knowledge as to how to adjust the whole piece of complicated machinery so that all the parts will work harmoniously. The smallest thing about your automobile is the spark. Without it the whole mass becomes junk. With the spark at least you can get the machinery to go, and you might plug along. But: Unless your spark is *timed* to fire at the exact moment when the piston reaches a certain point of elevation in the cylinder, you might as well get out and walk.

"It is the same way with the stock which you just mentioned. The company has ample working capital, high class management, big earning power, wonderful prospects. It is probably in a better and stronger position than when its stock sold thirty points higher. In this case the 'spark' is represented by the technical position. At 140 the spark was not properly adjusted. At 110 the adjustment has improved, but a study of the technical position of this stock will eventually point out the exact moment when it should be bought; so get all your other factors lined up ready for the time when the technical position shows that it is time to buy." In the fluctuations of almost every security there comes a time when it may be most advantageously bought or sold, and the training of one's judgment in the making of decisions as to "when," is one of the fine points in the business. It is also one of the least understood.

Certain "authorities" on securities and their markets have very frequently been proven to be badly wrong, principally because they have ignored this important consideration, They may as well ignore the trigger in a gun.

Carnegie's advice: "Put all your eggs in one basket and then watch the basket" might apply to an industrial organization of which he was the head, but it does not apply generally in the field of investment.

One's holdings should be so diversified by commitments in various lines of business, in different localities and subject to dissimilar influences, that no matter what happens, only a small portion of the investment is affected.

Before the Spanish War, our warships used to carry an observation tower which consisted of one solid piece of steel so constructed that a well-directed shot would demolish it, but during the war some bright mind in the navy conceived the idea of a tower consisting of a network of steel strips which took fifteen or more shots in certain spots to knock it down, and thus was the factor of safety vastly increased.

Investors should follow out this plan of protecting themselves by a diversification of investments, just as an insurance company avoids the risking of its capital and surplus on a single building. By spreading its risk over a vast number of buildings in various localities, it is protecting itself against a catastrophe.

Whatever the sum invested, it should be spread among at least ten to twenty different securities, greatly contrasting each other in nature of business, margin of safety, location of the industry, etc. Thus will your funds be hedged about with protection against shrinkage. And in the search for proper mediums you will widen your knowledge by a careful and discriminating study of the subject.

When you stop to think of it, you will see that it is impossible for all securities to have equal value and prospects; therefore some must be better than others. To be able to select the few which are absolutely the best requires a very broad knowledge and great statistical and analytical training and capability. The possession of such qualifications, however, enables one to go cross lots toward his goal of sound investments and money making.

XIV. IMPORTANCE OP KNOWING WHO OWNS A STOCK

IT is important to know whether large operators, inside interests, a pool, or the public dominate the market for a certain security or group.

You have often heard the expression, "Stocks are in weak hands." It is a matter of almost decisive importance to know where the stocks making up the leading group of speculative shares or any single security are held.

The reason this is so important is as follows: A combination of bankers will seldom be found on the long side of the market unless they expect a pronounced change in security market conditions in the near future. Their own purchases, therefore, are an indication of probable betterment. When a pool takes hold, it is usually in a certain one or a few issues which are likely to be favorably affected by developments known to a few but not generally known. The same is true of a large individual operator, who takes a position with a big line of stocks because he is confident that the future will cause others to take the securities off his hands at higher levels.

Operations on such a scale are very often the deciding factors in the trend of the market, because of the great quantities of securities which are dealt in. Such purchases exhaust the floating supply and thus lead to a higher level. Large interests and operators also have a way of influencing the market in the desired direction. This we may term manipulation, or advertising, or marking up, or whatever we choose, but it remains a fact, nevertheless, that this is frequently done. Some people claim that there is a "power" which dominates the market, and perhaps this is true to a degree, but not in the sense that many believe. Large interests sometimes work together, or observe each other's attitude by the action of their respective stocks, and thus operate in harmony, but without any actual understanding.

There is, however, another group of people operating in the market almost constantly, and this group is really the largest and most powerful of all. I refer to the investment and speculative public which is, in most cases, untrained, and as a body is unorganized. If the public could get together and operate in harmony so that it would not continually be stepping on its own toes, there would be a different kind of Wall Street; for without the public as a buffer, large interests, pools and operators would be comparatively powerless.

Some may criticize this statement on the ground that it is made offhand and without any definite proof, but I have had occasion in the past to prove that it is true, and do not consider it necessary to present the facts here. The report of the committee appointed m 1909 by Governor Hughes for the purpose of investigating the workings of the New York Stock Exchange, published in *The Magazine* for August, 1909, refers to the operations of the floor traders, who, "from their familiarity with the technique of dealings on the Exchange and their ability to act in concert with others and thus manipulate values, are supposed to have special advantages over other traders."

I claim that if a few floor traders, properly organized, can get results, the public could properly organized, control the situation. I merely mention this to illustrate the point that the big thing to know is where the stocks are, because the position of those who control is an indication of their attitude, pose and power.

It will be admitted that some years ago— before the railroads were persecuted and their profits curtailed by innumerable anti-railroad organizations—their securities were largely held by the great banking interests, each controlling its respective groups of securities. The Rockefellers were in St. Paul, New Haven and others, Harriman and Kuhn-Loeb interests in control of the Union Pacific, Southern Pacific, etc., and the Morgans dominated their specialties. But a change has come over the situation, and now I may safely make the statement that the great bulk of shares of the American railroads are in the hands of small investors.

Large interests got out long ago. They saw the "handwriting on the wall; they had a right to sell and protect themselves and they did sell. The big ten thousand, fifty thousand and hundred thousand share blocks were split up into small lots and are so held today. The ten share owner is now more representative of railroad control that at any time in the history of the world and this situation will continue until there is a very radical change in the outlook for the American railroad industry.

Having satisfied myself that this is the situation, I am in a better position to judge the action of the market for these stocks and to decide upon my individual course, so far as I care to trade or invest in the rails. There are exceptions to this rule, but it is safe to say that outside the individual movements in special issues or groups, there is not likely to be any concerted action until large interests see clearly that the future will be brighter and better, otherwise they would not be justified in accumulating.

When this accumulation begins, as it probably will, sooner or later, there will be a very distinct change in the character of the market for railroad stocks. That change will first evince itself in the transactions.

It will be seen from the above how important it is to know who holds the stocks, and how the public, unorganized, is incapable of applying anything but a superficial aid in the dull, dragging, declining markets we have had in this group.

This being the case, the bankers, large operators and pools, are looking elsewhere for their security market profits.

There are some opportunities that are better than any others offering at the moment. One's task is to ferret these out.

It is astonishing how many people in Wall Street work on "hunches." Whenever your friend tells you about the splendid profits he realized in certain transactions, he is almost certain to tell you, "I had a hunch that it was a purchase at that price." But when a loss results from some of his ventures, he does not lay it to a "hunch" but ta "hard luck."

People are apt to conduct their investments a good deal as advertising was conducted in former years, when the advertiser's theory was, "put an ad. in the paper and see how you come out." To quote from a very interesting address by Mr. M. H. Avram, "Advertising is no longer a hit or miss proposition—it is scientifically conducted and executed along previously determined and experience-proven lines. An advertising campaign may deviate at times as to details, due to circumstances that could not be for seen, but in its fundamentals the predetermined line is followed unwaveringly toward success."

In other words, advertising—formerly a very inexact science—has become scientific. It is quite within the bounds of possibility that investing may also be put on the same plane. We are making slow but steady progress toward that end.

In writing this book I have endeavored to give examples as to how some of the difficulties in this big subject can be overcome and the last few chapters have been devoted to observations which may help to solve some of these questions. I do not wish to close without saying a word in favor of the careful selection of investment mediums.

As stated at the beginning of this subject, there are some opportunities that are better than any others. When you stop to think of it, you will see that it is impossible for all securities to have equal value and prospects; therefore some must be better than others. To be able to select the few which are absolutely the best requires a very broad knowledge and great statistical and analytical training and capability. The possession of such qualifications, however, enables one to go cross-lots toward his goal of sound investments and moneymaking.

It is a deeply interesting subject. The more you learn, the more you realize how little you know, and the more anxious you become to acquire proficiency.

While as a nation we are perhaps becoming more studious, we are also more pleasure-loving. And one's desire to study and advance is often handicapped by the influences which pull him toward pastimes and recreation. An engineer friend of mine tells me that he never goes to sleep without reading on some educational subject for at least half an hour. This habit, now thoroughly formed, has been of inestimable value to him in his practice. His example may be imitated to very great advantage.

THE END

STUDIES IN TAPE READING

By RICHARD D. WYCKOFF
(Rollo Tape)

The Ticker Publishing Company, New York

CONTENTS

I. INTRODUCTORY

THERE is a widespread demand for more light on the subject of Tape Reading. Thousands of traders entertain the idea that in some way the market momentarily indicates its own immediate future; that these indications are accurately recorded on the tape; therefore he who can interpret what is imprinted on. the narrow paper ribbon has within his reach unlimited wealth.

Success of Tape Readers

It seems to me that such an opinion is fully warranted for *it is well known that many of the most successful traders and operators of the present day began operations by successful Tape Reading, trading in fractional lots of stock with a capital of only a few hundred dollars.*

Speaking of Joe Manning, one of the shrewdest and most successful of all the traders on the floor of the New York Stock Exchange, a friend of mine once said:

Joe Manning

"Joe and I used to trade in ten share lots together. He was an ordinary trader, just as I am. We used to hang over the same ticker."

The speaker was, at the time he made the remark, still trading in ten-share lots, while I happened to know that Joe's bank balance - his active working capital - amounted to $100,000, and that this represents but a part of the fortune built on his ability to interpret the language of the tape.

Why was one of these men able to amass a fortune, while the other never acquired more than a few thousand dollars at the same pursuit? Their chances were equal at the start so far as capital and opportunity go. The millions were there waiting to be won by either or both.

Mental Qualifications

The answer seems to be in the peculiar mental qualifications, highly potent in the successful trader, but unpossessed by the other.

There is, of course, a small element of luck in every case, but pure luck could not be so sustained in Manning's case as to carry him through operations covering a term of years.

By proper mental equipment we do not mean the mere ability to take a loss, define the trend, or to execute some other move characteristic of the professional trader. We refer to the active or dormant qualities in his make-up. The power to drill himself into the right mental attitude; to stifle his emotion, fear, anxiety, elation, recklessness, to train his mind into obedience so that it recognizes but one master - the tape - these, if possessed, would be as valuable in shaping the result as natural ability, or what is called the sixth sense in trading.

Some people are born musicians, others seemingly void of musical taste, *develop* themselves into virtuosos. It is the amount of I WILL in a man which makes him mediocre or pre-eminent - in Wall Street parlance, a dub or a big trader.

Jacob Field

Jacob Field is another exponent of Tape Reading. Those who knew "Jakey" when he began his Wall Street career, were impressed by his ability to read the tape, and follow the trend. His talent for this work was doubtless born in him; time and experience have intensified it until now he is considered by the majority of his fellows, the Prince of Floor Traders.

Jim Keene

Whatever laurels, Mr. Keene has won as an operator or syndicate manager, do not detract from his reputation as a Tape Reader. His scrutiny of the tape is so intense that he appears to be in a trance while his mental processes are being worked out. He seems to analyze prices, volumes and fluctuations down to the finest imaginable point, then telephones to the floor to ascertain the character of the buying or selling in . certain active stocks. With this auxiliary information he completes his judgment and makes his commitments.

Mr. Keene stands to-day on the pinnacle of fame as a Tape Reader, and his daily presence at the ticker is sufficient evidence that the work pays and pays well.

One might say: "These are rare examples. The average man never makes a success of Tape Reading."

Right you are! The *average* man seldom makes a success of anything.

Success in this field usually results from years of painstaking effort and absolute concentration upon the subject. It requires that one devote his whole time and attention to the tape. He should have no other business or profession.

"A man cannot serve two masters," and the tape is a tyrant.

Study Necessary

One cannot become a Tape Reader by giving the ticker absent treatment; nor by running into his broker's office after lunch, or seeing "how the market closed" from his evening newspaper. He cannot study this art from the far end of a telegraph or telephone wire. He should spend twenty-seven hours a week at the ticker, and many more hours away from it studying his mistakes and finding the "why" of his losses.

If Tape Reading were an exact science, one would simply have to assemble the factors, carry out the operations indicated, and trade accordingly. But the factors influencing the market are infinite in their number and character, as well as in their effect upon the market, and to attempt the construction of a Tape Reading formula would seem to be futile. However, something of the kind (in the rough) may develop as we progress in this investigation, so let us preserve open minds.

What is Tape Reading?

This question may be best answered by first deciding what it is not.

Tape Reading is not merely looking at the tape to ascertain how prices are running.

What Tape Reading is Not

It is not reading the news and then buying or selling "if the stock acts right."

It is not trading on tips, opinions, or information.

It is not buying "because they are going up," or selling "because they look weak."

It is not trading on chart indications or by other mechanical methods.

It is not "buying on dips-and selling on bulges."

Nor is it any of the hundred other foolish things practised by the millions of people without method, forethought or calculation.

Tape Reading Defined

Tape Reading seems to us: The science of determining from the tape the immediate trend of prices.

It is judging from what appears on the tape *now,* what is likely to be shown in five minutes or more.

It bears no relation to clairvoyancy and we do not believe that spirits of departed friends could be of assistance to students.

Tape Reading is rapid-fire horse sense. Its object is to determine whether Union Pacific, which is now 159, will sell at 160 before 158, or vice versa; to make deductions from each succeeding transaction - every shift of the market kaleidoscope; to grasp a new situation, force it lightning-like through the weighing machine of the brain, and to reach a decision which can be acted upon with coolness and precision - all within the space of a few seconds.

Supply and Demand

It is gauging the momentary supply and demand in particular stocks and in the whole market, comparing the forces behind each and their relationship, each to the other and to all.

A Tape Reader is like the manager of a department store; into his office are poured hundreds of reports of sales made by the various departments. He notes the general trend of business - whether demand is heavy or light throughout the store - but lends special attention to the lines in which demand is abnormally strong or weak. When he finds difficulty in keeping his shelves full in a certain department, he instructs his buyers, and 'they increase their buying orders; when certain goods do not move he knows there is little demand (market) for them, therefore, he lowers his prices - offers inducements to possible purchasers.

A floor trader who stands in one crowd all day is like the buyer for one department - he sees more quickly than anyone else the demand for that class of goods, but has no way of comparing it to that prevailing in other parts of the store.

He may be trading on the long side of Union Pacific, which has a strong upward trend, when suddenly a break in another stock will demoralize the market in Union Pacific, and he will be forced to compete with others who have stocks to sell.

Advantages of the Tape Reader

The Tape Reader, on the other hand, from his perch at the ticker, enjoys a bird's eye view of the whole field. When serious weakness develops in any quarter, he is quick to note, weigh and act.

Another advantage in favor of the Tape Reader: The tape tells the news minutes, hours and days before the news tickers, or newspapers, and before it- can become current gossip. Everything from a foreign war to the passing of a dividend; from a Supreme Court decision, to the ravages of the boll weevil is reflected primarily upon the tape.

The insider who knows a dividend is to be jumped from 6 per cent. to 10 per cent. shows his hand on the tape when he attempts to turn his knowledge into dollars, and the investor with 100 shares to sell makes his fractional impress upon its market price.

The market is like a slowly revolving wheel. Whether the wheel will continue to revolve in the same direction, stand still or reverse depends entirely upon the forces which come in contact with its hub and tread. Even when the contact is broken, and nothing remains to affect its course, the wheel retains a certain impulse from the most recent dominating force, and revolves until it comes to a standstill or is subjected to other influences.

The engineers who harnessed Niagara had a simple task compared to that of the Tape Reader. The cataract which he undertakes to control seemingly has cross-currents and maelstroms, reversing its direction and defying the laws of gravity. To divert a portion of this unruly Wall Street stream, to subject it to his will, seems like a task for a superman. Yet it can be done, for others have done it.

Manipulation

The element of manipulation need not discourage any one. Manipulators are giant traders, wearing seven-leagued boots. The trained ear can detect the steady "clump, clump," as they progress, and the footprints are recognized in enormous quantities of stock appearing on the tape. Little fellows are at liberty to tiptoe wherever the footprints lead, but they must be wary that the giants do not turn quickly and crush them.

The Tape Reader has many advantages over the long swing operator. He never ventures far from shore; that is, he plays with a close stop, never laying himself open to a large loss. Accidents or catastrophes cannot seriously injure him because he can reverse his position in an instant, and follow the new-formed stream from source to mouth. As his position on either the long or short side is confirmed and emphasized, he increases his line, thus following up and cumulating the advantage gained.

A Secure Position

A simon-pure Tape Reader does not care to carry stocks over night. The tape is then silent, and he only knows what to do when it tells him. Something may occur at midnight which may crumple up his diagram of the next day's market. He leaves nothing to chance; hence he prefers a clean sheet when the 3 o'clock gong strikes.

By this method interest charges are avoided, reducing the percentage against him to a considerable extent.

The Tape Reader is like a vendor of fruit who, each morning, provides himself with a stock of the choicest and mose seasonable products, and for which there is the greatest demand. He pays his cash and disposes of the goods as quickly as possible, at a profit varying from 50 to 100 per cent. on cost. To carry his stock over night causes a loss on account of spoilage. This corresponds with the interest charge to the trader.

The fruit vendor is successful because he knows what and when to buy, also where and how to sell. But there are stormy days when he cannot go out; when buyers do not appear; when he is arrested, fined, or locked up by a blue- coated despot or his wares are scattered abroad by a careless truckman.

Periods of Loss

Wall Street will readily apply these situations to the various attitudes in which the Tape Reader finds himself. He ventures $100 to make $200, and as the market goes in his favor his risk is reduced, but there are times when he finds himself at sea, with his stock deteriorating. Or the market is so unsettled that he does not know how to act; he is caught on stop or held motionless in a dead market; he takes a series of losses, or is obliged to be away from the tape when opportunities occur. His calculations are completely upset by some unforeseen event or his capital is impaired by overtrading or poor judgment.

The vendor does not hope to buy a barrel of apples for $3 and sell them the same day for $300. He expects to make from nothing to $3 a day. He depends upon a small but certain profit, which will average enough over a week or a month to pay him for his time and labor.

This is the objective point of the Tape Reader - to make an average profit. In a month's operations he may make $3,500 and lose $3,000 - a net profit of $500 to show for his work. If he can keep this average up, trading in 100-share lots, throughout a year, he has only to increase his unit to 200, 300, and 500 shares or more, and the results will be tremendous.

Average Profits

The amount of capital or the size of the order is of secondary importance to this question: Can you trade in and out of all kinds of markets and show an average profit of say ⅛ per cent. per day? If so, you are proficient in the art. If you can trade with only a small average loss per day, or come out even, you are rapidly getting there.

In the December TICKER there was set forth the record made by a trader whose operations showed 42 profits out of 71 trades, the gross points profit being 50⅜ against 37¼ gross points loss. This was good work, although the commissions and tax threw the net result over into a loss of 6 points. We mention this merely to show the standard by which success in Tape Reading should be measured.

The trader who there disclosed the outcome of his efforts was not a Tape Reader. He operated largely upon information and had no fixed method.

A Tape Reader abhors information and follows a definite and thoroughly tested plan, which after months and years of practice becomes second nature to him. His mind forms habits which operate automatically in guiding his market ventures.

No intelligent human need be told that when the sky darkens and the thunder rolls there's likely to be a shower. He unconsciously notes the preliminary signs, dons a raincoat and takes an umbrella.

Long practice will make the Tape Reader just as proficient in forecasting stock market events, but his intuition will be reinforced by logic, reason and analysis.

The Scalper

Here we find the characteristics which distinguish the Tape Reader from the Scalper. The latter is essentially one who tries to grab a point or two profit "without rhyme or reason" - he don't care how, so long as he gets it.

A Scalper will trade on a tip, a look, a guess, a hearsay, on what he thinks or what a friend of a friend of Morgan's says.

The Tape Reader evolves himself into an automaton which takes note of a situation, weighs it, decides upon a course and gives an order. There is no. quickening of the pulse, no nerves, no hopes or fears. The result produces neither elation nor depression. There is equanimity before," during and after the trade.

The Scalper is a bob-tailed car with rattling windows, a jouncing motion and a strong tendency to jump the track.

The Tape Reader is like a Pullman coach, which travels smoothly and steadily along the roadbed of the tape, acquiring direction and speed from the market engine, and being influenced by nothing else whatever.

Qualifications of a Tape Reader

Having thus described our ideal Tape Reader in a general way, let us inquire into some of the requisite qualifications.

First, he must be absolutely self-reliant. A dependent person whose judgment hangs upon that of others will find himself swayed by a thousand outside influences. At critical points his judgment will be useless. He must be able to say: "The facts are – ; the resulting indications are – ; therefore I will do thus and so."

Next he must be familiar with the technicalities of the market, so that every little incident affecting prices will be given due weight. He should know the history, earnings and financial condition of the companies in whose stock he is trading; the ways of the manipulators; the different kinds of markets; be able to measure the effect of news and rumors; know when and in what stocks it is best to trade; measure the forces behind them; know when to cut a loss and take a profit.

Knowledge of Market

He must study the various swings and know where the market and his particular stock stand; must recognize the inherent weakness or strength of the market; understand the basis or logic of movements. He should study the fundamentals and sift the wheat from the chaff; recognize the turning points of the market; see in his mind's eye what is happening on the floor.

Nerve and Patience Seclusion

He must have the nerve to stand a series of losses; persistence to keep him at the work during adverse periods; selfcontrol to avoid overtrading and a phlegmatic disposition to ballast and balance him at all times.

For perfect concentration as a protection from the tips, gossip and other influences which abound in a broker's office, he should, if possible, seclude himself. A tiny room with a ticker, a desk and private telephone connection with his broker's office are all the facilities required. The work requires such delicate balance of the faculties that the slightest influence either way may throw the result against the trader. He may say: "Nothing influences me," but unconsciously it does affect his judgment to know that another man is bearish at a point where he thinks stocks should be bought. The mere thought, "He may be right," has a deterring influence upon him; he hesitates; the opportunity is lost. No matter how the market goes from that point, he has missed a cog and his mental machinery is thrown out of gear. Silence is a much needed lubricant to the Tape Reader's mind.

The advisability of having even a news ticker in the room, is a subject for discussion.

The tape tells the present and future of the market.

The news ticker records what *has* happened. It announces the cause for the effect which has already been more or less felt in the market.

Money is made in Tape Reading by anticipating what is coming - not by waiting till it happens and going with the crowd.

News

The *effect* of news is an entirely different proposition. Considerable light is thrown on the technical strength or weakness of the market and special stocks by their action in the face of important news. For the moment it seems to us that a news ticker might be admitted to the sanctum, provided its whisperings are given only the weight to which they are entitled.

To evolve a practical method - one which *any* trader may use in his daily operations and which those with varying proficiency in the art of Tape Reading will find of value and assistance - such is the task we have set before us in this series. Perhaps we shall succeed; perhaps not.

Our Task

We will consider all the market factors of vital importance in Tape Reading, as well as methods used by experts. These will be illustrated by reproductions from the tape. Every effort will be made to produce something of definite, tangible value to those who are now operating in a hit-or-miss sort of way.

II.
PRELIMINARY SUGGESTIONS

Actual Trading Necessary

WHEN embarking on any new enterprise, the first thing to consider is the amount of capital required. To study Tape Reading "on paper" is one thing, but to practice and become proficient in the art is quite another. Almost anyone can make money on imaginary trades, for these require no risk of any kind - the mind is free from the strain which accompanies an actual venture; fear does not enter into the situation; patience is unlimited.

All this is changed when even a small market commitment is made. The trader of slight experience suffers mental anguish if the stock does not instantly go his way; he is afraid of a large loss, hence his judgment becomes warped, and he closes the trade in order to secure mental relief.

As these are all symptoms of inexperience, they cannot be overcome by avoiding the issue. The brave and the business-like thing to do is to wade right into the game and learn to play it under conditions which are to be met and conquered before success can be attained.

Start Small

After a complete absorption of every available piece of educational writing bearing upon Tape Reading, it is best to commence trading in ten share lots, so as to acquire genuine trading experience. This may not suit some people with a propensity for gambling, and who look upon the ten-share trader as a piker. The average lamb with $10,000 wants to commence with 100 to 500- share lots - he wishes to start at the top and work down. It is only a question of time when he will have to trade in ten-share lots.

To us it seems better to start at the bottom with ten shares. There is plenty of time in which to increase the unit if you are successful. If success is not eventually realized you will be many dollars better off for having ventured the minimum quantity.

It has already been shown in The Ticker's Inquiry Column that the market for odd lots on the New York Stock Exchange is most satisfactory, so there is no other excuse for the novice who desires to trade in round lots than greed-of-gain, or get-rich-quick. Think of a baby, just learning to walk, being entered in a race with professional sprinters!

Points, Not Dollars

In the previous chapter we suggested that success in Tape Reading should be measured by the number of *points* profit over *points* lost. For all practical purposes, therefore, we might trade in one-share lots, were there no objection on the part of our broker, and if this quantity were not so absurdly small as to invite careless executions. Ten shares is really the smallest quantity that should be considered, but we mention one share simply to impress upon our readers that in studying Tape Reading, better keep in mind that you are playing for *points,* not dollars. The dollars will come along fast enough if you can make more points *net* than you lose. The professional billiardist playing for a stake aims to *out-point* his antagonist. After trading for a few months do not consider the dollars you are ahead or behind, but analyze the record in points. In this way your progress may be studied.

Capital

As the initial losses in trading are likely to be heavy, and as the estimated capital must be a more or less arbitrary amount, we should say that units of $1,000 would be necessary for each ten- share' lot traded in at the beginning. This allows for 90 points more losses than profits, and still leaves margin with which to proceed. Some people will secure a footing with less capital; others may be obliged to put up several units of $1,000 each before they begin to show profits; still others will spend a fortune (large or small) without making it pay, or meeting with any encouragement.

Look over R. G. Dun & Co.'s Causes of Commercial Failures, as recently tabulated in this magazine, and you will find the chief causes to be: (1) Lack of capital, and (2) Incompetence.

Causes of Failure

Lack of capital in Wall Street operations can usually be traced to over-trading. This bears out the epigram "Over-trading is financial suicide." It may mean too large a quantity of stock in the initial operations, or if the trader loses money, he may not reduce the size of his trade to- correspond with the shrinkage in his capital.

Over-Trading

To make our point clear: A man starts trading in 100-share lots on 20 points margin. After a series of losses he finds that he has only $200 remaining. This is still 20 points on ten shares, but does he reduce his orders? No. He risks the $200 on a 50 or 100-share trade in a last desperate effort to recoup. After being wiped out he tells his friends how he "could have made money if he had had more capital."

Ignorance

Incompetence really deserves first place in the list. Supreme ignorance is the predominant feature of both Wall Street lamb and seasoned speculator. It is surprising how many people stay in the Street year after year, acquiring nothing more, apparently, than a keen scent for tips and gossip. Ask them a technical question that smacks of scientific knowledge of the tape, and they are unable to reply.

Such folks are there for one of two reasons: They have either been "lucky" or their margins are replenished from some source outside of Wall Street.

The proportion of commercial failures due to Lack of Capital or Incompetence is about 60 per cent. Call the former by its Wall Street cognomen - Overtrading - and the percentage of stock market disasters traceable thereto would be about 90.

Success is only for the few, and the problem is to ascertain, with the minimum expenditure of time and money, whether you are fitted for the work.

Vital Questions

These, in a nutshell, are the vital questions up to this point:

Have you technical knowledge of the market and the factors which move it?

Have you $1,000 or more which you can afford to lose in an effort to demonstrate your ability at Tape Reading ?

Can you devote your entire time and attention to the study and the practice of this science?

Are you so fixed financially that you are not dependent upon your possible profits, and so that you will not suffer if none are forthcoming now or later?

There is no sense in mincing words over this matter, nor in holding out false encouragement to people who are looking for an easy, drop-a-penny-in- the-slot way of making money. Tape Reading is hard work, hence those who are mentally lazy need not apply.

Choice of Brokers

Nor should anyone to whom it will mean worry as to where his bread and butter is coming from. Money-worry is not conducive to clear-headedness. Over-anxiety upsets the equilibrium of a trader more than anything else. So if you cannot afford the time and money, and have not the necessary supply of patience, better wait. Start right or not at all.

Having decided to proceed, the trader who is equal to the foregoing circumstances finds himself asking, "Where shall I trade?"

The choice of a broker is an important matter to the Tape Reader. He should find one especially equipped for the work: who can give close attention to his orders, furnish quick bid and asked prices, and other technical information, such as the quantities wanted and offered at different levels, etc. The broker most to be desired should never have so much business on hand that he cannot furnish the trader with a verbal flashlight of what the crowd in this or that stock is doing, at any particular moment. This is important, for at times it will be money in the pocket to know just in what momentary position one stock or the market stands. The broker who is not over-burdened with business can give this service; he can also devote time and care to the execution of orders.

Handling an Order

Let me give an instance of how this works out in practice: You are long 100 Union, with a stop-order just under the market price; a dip comes and 100 shares sells at your stop price - say 164. Your careful, and not too busy broker stands in the crowd. He observes that several thousand shares are bid for at 164 and only a few hundred offered at the price. He does not sell the stock, but waits to see if it won't rally. It does rally. You are given a new lease of life. This handling of the order may benefit you $50, $100 or several hundred dollars in each instance, and is an advantage to be sought when choosing a broker.

The house which transacts an active commission business for a large clientele is unable to give this service. Its stop- orders and other orders not "close to the market," must be given to Specialists, and the press of business is such that it cannot devote especial attention to the orders of any one client. Hence, it would seem that our Tape Reader had better search for a small commission house which has one New York Stock Exchange member, an office partner and only one or two employees.

The number of clerks is a good index to the amount of business done. Their fewness is not a reflection on the strength, standing, or brokerage ability of the house. Some people are good brokers and have ample capital, but they do not understand the science of business getting.

Small House Best

In a small house, such as we have described the Tape Reader is less likely to be bothered by a gallery of traders, with their diverse and loud-spoken opinions. In other words, he will be left more or less to himself and be free to concentrate upon his task.

The ticker should be within calling distance of the telephone to the Stock Exchange. Some brokers have a way of making you or a clerk walk a mile to give an order. Every step means delay. The elapse of a few seconds may result in a lost market or opportunity. If you are in a small private room away from the order desk, there should be a special telephone connecting you with the order clerk. Ponderous, ice-wagon methods won't go in Tape Reading.

Orders should generally be given "at the market." We make this statement as a result of long experience and observation, and believe we can demonstrate the advisability of it.

The process of reporting transactions on the tape, as recently set forth. in these pages, consumes from five seconds to say five minutes, depending upon the activity of the market. For argument's sake, let us consider that the *average* interval between the time a sale takes place on the floor and the report appears on the tape is half a minute.

Giving Orders

A market order in an active stock is usually executed and reported to the customer in about two minutes. Half this time is consumed in putting your broker into the crowd with the order in hand; the other half in writing out and transmitting the report. Hence, when Union Pacific comes 164 on the tape and you instantly decide to buy it, the period of time between your decision and the execution of your order is as follows:

	Minutes.
The tape is behind the market	½
Time elapsed before broker can execute the order	1
	1½

It will therefore be seen that your decision is based on a price which prevailed half a minute ago, and that you must purchase if you will, at the price at which the stock stands one minute hence.

This might happen between your decision and the execution of your order:

UP 164. ⅛. ¼. ⅜. ½. ¼. ⅛. 164,

and yours might be the last hundred. When the report arrived you could not swear that it was bought at 164 before or after it touched 164½. Or you might get it at 164½, even though it was 164 when you gave the order, and when the report was handed to you.

Just as often the opposite will take place – the stock will go in your favor. In fact, the thing averages up in the long run, so that traders who do not give market orders are hurting their own chances.

Limited Orders

An infinite number of traders, seeing Union Pacific at 164, will say:

"Buy me a hundred at 164."

The broker who is not too busy will go into the crowd, and, finding the stock at 164⅛@¼ will report back to the office that "Union is ⅛ bid."

The trader gives his broker no credit for this service; instead, he considers it a sign that his broker, the floor traders and the insiders have all conspired to make him pay ¼ Per cent. higher for his 100 shares, so he replies:

"Let it stand at 164. If they don't give it to me at that, I won't buy it at all."

How foolish! Yet characteristic of the style of reasoning used by the public. His argument is that the stock, for good and sufficient reasons, is a splendid purchase at 164. At 164⅛ or ¼ these reasons are completely nullified; the stock becomes dear, or he cares more to foil the plans of this "band of robbers" than for a possible profit.

If a stock is cheap at 164 it's cheap at 164¼.

If you can't trust your broker, get another.

If you think the law of supply and demand is altered to catch your $25, better reorganize your thinkery.

On the Floor

Were you on the floor you could probably buy at 164 the minute it touched that figure, but of this there is no certainty. You would, however, be 1½ minutes nearer to the market. Your commission charges would also be practically eliminated. Therefore, if you have seventy or eighty thousand dollars lying around the house which you do not especially need, buy a seat. If you have not, cease the uproar.

A Tape Reader who deserves the name, makes money in spite of commissions, taxes and delays.'

Arthur Livermore

Arthur Livermore used to trade solely on what the tape told him, closing out everything before three o'clock. He traded from an office and paid the regular commissions, yet three trades out of five showed profits. Having made a fortune, he invested it in bonds and gave them all to his wife. Anticipating the 1907 panic, he put his $13,000 automobile up for a loan of $5,000, and with this capital started to play the bear side, using his profits as additional margin. At one time he was short 70,000 shares of Union Pacific. His whole line was covered on one of the panic days, and his net profits were a million dollars!

Get on Board!

To return to the question of giving orders: Anyone who says, "This stock should be bought but I will not pay ⅛ above my price for it," is like a man who thinks he can make certain money if he could but get to Chicago. Arriving at the ticket office he finds that the fare is $2 more than he expected, but though well heeled, he refuses to pay the required amount and abandons the trip.

If you don't get aboard your train, you'll never arrive.

Giving limited orders loses more good dollars than it saves. We refer, of course, to orders in the big, active stocks, wherein the bid and asked prices are usually ⅛ apart. Especially is this true in closing out a trade. Many foolish people are interminably hung up because they try to save eighths by giving limited orders in a market that is running away from them.

For the Tape Reader there is a psychological moment when he must open or close his trade. His orders must therefore be "at the market." Haggling over fractions will make him lose the thread of the tape, upset his poise and interrupt the workings of his mental machinery.

Scale Trading

In scale buying or selling it is obvious that limited orders must be used. There are certain other times when they are of advantage, but as the Tape Reader generally goes with the trend it is a case of "get on or get left."

By all means "get on."

Selection of Stocks

This is an important matter, and should be decided in a general way before one starts to trade. Let's nose around a little and see what we can reason out.

If you are trading in 100-share lots, your stock must move your way one point to make $100 profit.

Which class of stocks are most likely to move a point? Answer: The high-priced issues.

Looking over the records we find that a stock selling around 150 will average 2½ points fluctuation a day, while one selling at 50 will average only one point. Consequently, you have 2½ times more action in the higher priced stock.

The commission and tax charges are the same in both. Interest charges are three times as large, but this is an insignificant item to the Tape Reader who closes out his trades each day.

The higher priced stocks also cover a greater number of points during the year or cycle than those of lower price - Union Pacific from 195⅜ down to par (95⅜ points), against Steel common from 50⅜ down to 21⅞ (28½ points) being recent striking examples. Stocks like Great Northern, although enjoying a much wider range, are not desirable for trading purposes when up to 300 or more - fluctuations and bid and asked prices are too far apart to permit rapid in-and-out trading.

Important Stocks

The trend of the general market is largely made by the following stocks, in the order named:

Union Pacific
Reading
Steel Common
St. Paul
Amalgamated
Smelters

Union Pacifi

Union Pacific is the leader because it is the pivotal stock of the Harriman group, there is a large floating supply, a broad market and wide swings; it is popular with floor traders, big and little. Southern Pacific is its running mate, but owing to the smaller number of shares of the latter afloat, it seldom disputes for the leadership. The speculative possibilities in Union Pacific are so enormous, and the methods of Harriman and his associates so calculated to keep the public on tip-toe that the stock responds instantly to every wave of sentiment.

Reading

Reading from the top to the bottom of the last swing (164 to 70½) made 94½ points, practically the same as Union Pacific. Its daily swings also about correspond. There is only $70,- 000,000 of it outstanding. The floating supply is small, owing to the large blocks that are held by other roads, or by permanent investors. Hence, it is easy to manipulate. The comparative scarcity of the stock is shown in the frequency of ¼ point fluctuations between sales.

It is a very satisfactory stock for Tape Reading operations.

U. S. Steel

Steel common is lumbering in its movements, thus reflecting the five million shares outstanding and the consequent widespread public interest. It is useful as a barometer of the market and of public sentiment, but its swings, are rarely wide enough for the Tape Reader, as they average only about a point a day.

St. Paul

St. Paul is one of the truest stocks for trading purposes. It is manipulated at times, but generally it responds automatically to the slightest change in market temper. Its daily movements are wide, about equal to Union Pacific and Reading. Its last big swing was 106 points.

Amalgamated Copper

Amalgamated is at present only a secondary leader, and taking the year through not nearly as satisfactory to deal in as some of the others above mentioned. Its swing in 1907 was about 80 points.

Smelters

Smelters is one of the most highly manipulated issues on the list, erratic, often difficult to follow, at other times easy. Its daily range is usually equal to any of the others, and its last big swing was about 116 points. One gets plenty of action in Smelters, but not nearly the steadiness, nor the clearly defined trend prevailing in the big railroads.

Best Stocks for the Tape Reader

As a result of observation and years of trading experience, we prefer Union Pacific to any other, because of the qualities to which we have referred. In its present range (between 160 and 170) it is below the price warranted by its dividend rate and equities. This makes it especially responsive to bullish news and better adapted for trading on the long side.

If obliged to choose a second stock, Reading would appeal to us as offering the next greatest advantages. While Reading contains enormous intrinsic value it is at present a 4 per cent. stock selling in the 130s - a price scarcely warranted if its rate were increased to 5 per cent. So, for the time being at least, Reading affords the best medium for short selling.

These two issues are the chief hinges on which the door of the market turns - Union the upper, Reading the lower hinge. It is unnecessary for anyone to go beyond these except in times when the industrials dominate the market; in this case, Amalgamated, Smelters or Steel will replace them temporarily.

Trade in One Stock at a Time

It is better for a Tape Reader to trade in one stock than two or more. Stocks have habits and characteristics which are as distinct as those of human beings or animals. By a close study the trader becomes intimately acquainted with these habits and is able to anticipate the stock's action under given circumstances. A stock may be stubborn, sensitive, irresponsive, complaisant, aggressive; it may dominate the tape or trail along behind the rest; it is whimsical and coquettish; it may whisper, babble like a brook or roar like a cataract. Its moods must be studied if you would know it and bend it to your will.

Study implies concentration. A person who trades in a dozen stocks at a time cannot concentrate on one.

The popular method of trading (which means the unsuccessful way) is to say:

"I think the market's a sale. Smelters, Copper and St. Paul have had the biggest rise lately; they ought to have a good reaction; sell a hundred of each for me."

Concentrate

Trades based on thinks seldom pan out well. The selection of two or three stocks by guesswork instead of one by reason and analysis explains many of the public's losses. If a trader wishes to trade in three hundred shares, let him sell that quantity of the stock which he knows most about, or which is entitled to the greatest decline. Unless he is playing the long swing he injures his chances by trading in a lot of stocks at once. It's like chasing a drove of pigs - while you're watching this one the others get away.

Better to concentrate on one or two stocks and study them exhaustively. You will find that what applies to one does not always fit the other: each must be judged on its own merits. The varying price levels, volumes, percentage of floating supply, investment values, the manipulation and other factors, all tend to produce a different combination in each particular case.

III.
THE STOCK LIST ANALYZED

The Best Stock Now

IN the last chapter we referred to Union Pacific as the most desirable stock for active trading. The "Analyst" informs us that he once made a composite chart of the principal active stocks, for the purpose of ascertaining which, in its daily fluctuations, followed the course of the general market most accurately. He found Union Pacific was what might be called the market backbone, while the others, especially Reading, frequently showed erratic tendencies, running up or down, more or less contrary to the general trend. Of all the issues under inspection, none possessed the all-around steadiness and general desirability for trading purposes displayed by Union Pacific.

But the Tape Reader, even if he decides to operate exclusively in one • stock, cannot close his eyes to what is going on in others. Frequent opportunities occur elsewhere. In proof of this, take the market in the early fall of 1907: Union Pacific was the leader throughout the rise from below 150 to 167⅝. For three or four days before this advance culminated, heavy selling occurred in Reading, St. Paul, Copper, Steel and Smelters, under cover of the strength in Union. This made the turning point of the market as clear as daylight. One had only to go short of Reading and await the break, or he could have played Union with a close stop, knowing that the whole market would collapse as soon as Union turned downward. When the liquidation in other stocks was completed, Union stopped advancing, the supporting orders were withdrawn, and the "pre-election break" took place. This amounted to over 20 points in Union, with proportionate declines in the rest of the list.

View the Market Broadly

The operator who was watching only Union would have been surprised at this; but had he viewed the market as a complete organism he must have seen what was coming. Knowing the point of distribution, he would be on the lookout for the accumulation which must follow, or at least the level where support would be forthcoming. Had he been expert enough to detect this, quick money could have been made on the subsequent rally.

While Union Pacific at present constitutes the backbone, this important member is only one part of the market body, which after all is very like the physical structure of a human being..

To get this point clearly in mind, let us draw on our imaginations a little: Union is strong and advancing; suddenly New York Central develops an attack of gout; Consolidated Gas goes off on a spree; American Ice becomes nauseatingly weak; Southern Railway develops typhoid; Great Western cannot meet expenses, and is prostrated. There may be nothing at all the matter with the backbone, but its strength will be affected by sickness or excesses among the other members.

Sympathetic Movements

A bad break may come in Brooklyn Rapid Transit, occasioned by some political attack, or other purely local influence. This cannot possibly affect the business of the grangers, transcontinentals, or coalers, yet St. Paul, Union, and Reading decline as much as B. R. T. A person whose finger is crushed will sometimes faint from the shock to his nervous system, although the injured member will in no wise affect the other members or functions of the body.

The time-worn illustration of the chain which is as strong as its weakest link, will not serve. When the weak link breaks the chain is in two parts, each part being as strong as its weakest link. The market does not break in two, even when it receives a severe blow. If something occurs in the nature of disaster, whereby the money situation, investment demand, public sentiment, and corporate earning power are deeply affected, a tremendous break may occur, but there is always a level, even in a panic, where buying power becomes strong enough to produce a rally or a permanent upturn.

The Tape Reader must endeavor to operate in that stock which combines the widest swings with the broadest market; he may therefore frequently find it to his advantage to switch temporarily into other issues which seem to offer the quickest and surest profits. It is necessary for us to become familiar with the characteristics of the principal speculative mediums that we may judge their advantages in this respect, as well as their weight and bearing upon a given market situation.

The Market is Mental

The market is made by the minds of many men. The state of these minds is reflected in the prices of securities in which their owners operate. Let us examine some of the individuals, as well as the influences behind certain stocks and groups of stocks in their various relationships. This will, in a sense, enable us to measure their respective power to affect the whole list or the specific issue in which we decide to operate.

The market leaders are, as already stated, Union, Reading, Steel, St. Paul, Amalgamated and Smelters. Manipulators, professionals and the public derive their inspiration largely from the action of these six issues, in which 40 per cent to 80 per cent of the total daily transactions are concentrated. We will therefore designate these as the "Big Six."

The Big Six

Four stocks out of the Big Six are chiefly influenced by the operations of what is known as the Harriman-Standard Oil party, the most active members of which are E. H. Harriman, William Rockefeller, H. H. Rogers, and H. C. Frick. Their four stocks are Union, Reading, St. Paul, and Amalgamated. Of the other two, Smelters is handled by the Guggenheims, while Steel is unquestionably swung up and down more by the influence of public sentiment than anything else. Of course the condition of the steel trade forms the basis of important movements in this issue, and occasionally Morgan or some other large interest may take a hand by buying or selling a few hundred thousand shares, but, generally speaking, it is the attitude of the public which chiefly affects the price of Steel common. This should be borne strictly in mind, as it is a valuable guide to the technical position of the market, which frequently turns on the over-bought or oversold condition of the public.

Next in importance come what we will term the Secondary Leaders; viz., those which at times burst into great activity, accompanied by large volume. These are rightly termed Secondary Leaders, because while they seldom influence the Big Six to a marked extent, the less important issues usually fall into line at their initiative.

Secondary Leaders

The principal Secondary Leaders are:

Atchison
Baltimore & Ohio
Brooklyn Rapid Transit
Colorado Fuel
Consolidated Gas
Delaware & Hudson
Erie
Great Northern
Northern Pacific
Illinois Central
Louisville & Nashville
Missouri Pacific
New York Central
Pennsylvania
Southern Pacific
Sugar

Minor Stocks

Another group which we will call the Minor Stocks is comprised of less important issues, mostly low-priced, and embracing many public favorites, such as

American Car & Foundry
Chesapeake & Ohio
Chicago Great Western
Colorado Southern
Denver & Rio Grande

Interborough
Mexican Central
Missouri, Kansas & Texas
Norfolk & Western
Ontario & Western
Republic Iron & Steel
Rock Island
Southern Railway'
Texas Pacific
Wabash

Minor Stocks Do Not Lead

These groups are arranged solely with regard to their present speculative prominence, and their power to influence the general market. Some people, when they see an advance inaugurated in some of the Minor Stocks, such as Chesapeake & Ohio, Ontario & Western, or Rock Island, are led to buy Pennsylvania, Reading and other Primary or Secondary Leaders, on the ground that the latter will be bullishly affected. This sometimes occurs; more often it does not. It is just as fallacious to expect a 5,000-share operator to follow a 100-share trader, or a 100-share man to be influenced by what the 10-share trader is doing.

The various stocks in the market are like a gigantic fleet of boats, all hitched together and being towed by the tugs "Money Situation," and "Business Conditions." In the first row of boats are the Big Six; behind them, the Secondary Leaders, the Minors, and the Miscellaneous issues in the order named. It takes time to generate steam and to get the fleet under way. The leaders are first to feel the impulse; the others follow in turn. Should the tugs halt, the fleet will run along for awhile under its own momentum, and there will be a certain amount of bumping, backing and filling. In case the direction of the tugs is changed abruptly, the bumping is apt to be severe. Obviously, those in the rear cannot gain and hold the leadership without an all-around readjustment.

The Big Six are representative of America's greatest industries - railroading, steel making, and mining. It is but natural that these stocks should form the principal outlet to the country's speculative tendencies. The Union Pacific and St. Paul systems cover the entire West. Reading, of itself a large railroad property, dominates the coal mining industry; it is so interlaced with other railroads as to typify the Eastern situation. Steel is closely bound up with the state of general business throughout the states, while Amalgamated and Smelters are the controlling factors in copper mining and the smelting industry.

Groups

In order that we may consider the relationships of the principal stocks on the list, let us further divide the active issues into groups.

THE HARRIMAN GROUP.[1]

Union Pacific, Reading, Southern Pacific, Atchison, Erie, Illinois Central, Pacific Mail, Wheeling and Lake Erie.

THE STANDARD OIL GROUP.

Amalgamated Copper, Anaconda, Sugar, St. Paul, Consolidated Gas, Corn Products, American Linseed, Brooklyn Union Gas.

THE MORGAN GROUP.

Atlantic Coast Line, Hocking Valley, Louisville & Nashville, Southern Railway, U. S. Steel, General Electric, and Mercantile Marine.

THE PENNSYLVANIA GROUP.*

Pennsylvania, Pittsburg, Cin. Ch. & St. Louis, Baltimore & Ohio, Chesapeake & Ohio, Norfolk & Western.

THE HILL GROUP.

Great Northern, Northern Pacific, Great Northern Ore & Pacific Coast.

THE GOULD GROUP

Missouri Pacific, Denver & Rio Grande, Texas Pacific, Wabash, Western Maryland, St. Louis Southwestern, Western Union, and Colorado Fuel.

THE VANDERBILT GROUP.

New York Central, Northwest, C., C., C., & St. L.; Lake Erie & Western, N. Y., Chicago & St. L., N. Y. & Harlem, and Delaware & Hudson.

---

[1] The death of Mr. Harriman since the above has changed these groups somewhat.

THE HAWLEY GROUP[2].

Colorado & Southern, Minneapolis & St. Louis, Iowa Central, Toledo, St. L. & Western, Chicago & Alton.

THE MOORE GROUP.

Rock Island, St. L. & San Francisco, American Can.

THE CANADIAN PACIFIC GROUP.

Canadian Pacific, Minneapolis, St. Paul, S. S. Marie, Duluth, South Shore & Atlantic.

*

THE GUGGENHEIM GROUP.

Am. Smelting, National Lead, Utah Copper.

THE NEW HAVEN GROUP.

New Haven, Ontario & Western.

Arranged according to industries we have the following:

STEEL STOCKS.

U. S. Steel, Am. Steel Foundries, Bethlehem Steel, Colorado Fuel & Iron, Great Northern Ore, Republic Iron & Steel, Sloss-Sheffield, U. S. Cast Iron Pipe & Foundry.

EQUIPMENT STOCKS.

Am. Car & Foundry, Am. Locomotive, N. Y. Air Brake, Pressed Steel Car, Pullman, Railway Steel Springs.

ELECTRICAL STOCKS.

General Electric, Westinghouse, Allis- Chalmers.

COPPER STOCKS.

Amalgamated, Anaconda, Granby, Newhouse, Tennessee, Utah (Am. Smelters is also closely identified with this industry).

TELEGRAPH AND TELEPHONE STOCKS.

Western Union, Mackay Companies, Am. Telegraph & Telephone.

ANTHRACITE STOCKS.

Reading, Erie, Delaware, Lack. & Western, Delaware & Hudson, Ontario & Western, and Pennsylvania.

CHEMICAL STOCKS.

Am. Agricultural Chemical, Virginia- Carolina Chemical, Am. Cotton Oil.

---

2 Chesapeake & Ohio has since become a Hawley property.

The above are the principal groups. There are, of course, a number of independent railroads, such as Missouri, Kansas & Texas, Kansas City Southern, Chicago Great Western, and* Wisconsin Central, besides local traction companies and combines, such as the Ryan- Belmont Group in New York City, including Interborough-Metropolitan, Third Avenue, and Manhattan. These and other public utility stocks, such as Peoples Gas, and Toledo Railway & Light, etc., are governed by local conditions, and do not, as a rule, affect the general list.

Industrials

Large industrial concerns like Am. Sugar, Am. Woolen, International Paper, International Harvester, U. S. Rubber, etc., are also affected principally by the state of their respective trades, and carry little weight otherwise.

Sympathetic Relations

Having classified the principal active stocks we can now recognize more clearly the forces behind their movements. For instance, if Consolidated Gas suddenly becomes strong and active, we know it will probably affect Brooklyn Union Gas, but there is no reason why the other Standard Oil stocks should advance more than slightly and out of sympathy. But if all the stocks in the Standard Oil group advance in a steady and sustained fashion, we know that these capitalists are engaged in a bull campaign. As these people do not enter deals for a few points it is safe to go along with them for awhile, or until distribution becomes apparent.

An outbreak of speculation in Colorado Fuel is no bull argument on the other Steel stocks. It usually means that the Gould party is active. If it were based "on trade conditions, U. S. Steel would be the first to feel the impetus, which would radiate to the others.

In selecting the most desirable stock out of the Standard Oil group, for instance, the Tape Reader must consider whether conditions favor the greatest activity and volumes in the railroad or industrial field. In the former case, his choice would be St. Paul; in the latter, Amalgamated.

A Low-Priced Stock Rarely Leads

In the Harriman Group, Erie may come out of its rut (as it did during the summer of 1907, when it was selling around 24), and attain leadership among the low-priced stocks. This indicates some important development in Erie; it does not foreshadow a rise in all the Harrimans. But if a strong rise starts in Union Pacific, and Southern Pacific and the others in the group follow consistently, the Tape Reader will get into the leader and stay with it. He will not waste time on Erie, for while it is moving up 5 points, Union Pacific will advance 10 or 15 points, provided it is a genuine Harriman move. Many valuable deductions may be made by studying these groups.

Experience has shown that when a rise commences in Atchison (a Secondary Leader), the Big Six is about done and distribution is taking place, under protection of the strength in Atchison and others in its class. Sugar acts in a similar capacity for the Standard Oil group. Professional traders call these stocks "Indicators."

Indicators

The Harriman and Standard Oil parties work in harmony, their relations in the various properties being closely interwoven.

The Morgan people are comparatively inactive, except at times when they turn over immense quantities of Steel securities. We feel safe in asserting that few manipulative orders emanate from the corner of Wall and Broad. This is also true of the Hill and Pennsylvania groups, except in rare instances, when bankers are bringing out new issues.

Pools

The absence of inside manipulation in a stock leaves the way open for pools to operate, and many of the moves that are observed in these groups are produced by a handful of floor or office operators, who, by joining hands and swinging large quantities, are able to force their stock in the desired direction.

Activity in the Gould group is largely confined to Missouri Pacific and Colorado Fuel, but the others are taken in hand at times, with the exception of Western Union, which is principally held for investment.

Of the Vanderbilts, New York Central is the leader; all the others usually take their cue from it. Neglect is the principal market characteristic of the majority of this group, most of the outstanding shares being locked up in safe deposit boxes. The principal moves are made by those not identified with the Vanderbilts. (It will be noted that Wm. Rockefeller, James Stillman, and some of the Morgan party are directors.) The "Junior" Vanderbilts, such as N. Y., Ch., & St L., and Lake Erie & Western are poor leaders, and generally unsatisfactory stocks to watch, except as straws, showing the direction of the wind.

Subordinate Groups

With the exception of Chesapeake & Ohio and Colorado & Southern, the Hawley stocks cut very little figure – their movements carry slight significance.

The Moore party's principal activities are confined to Rock Island, the influence of which seldom extends beyond its own controlled properties.

The primary market for Canadian Pacific is in London. The movements of its American loop (Minn., St Paul & S. S. Marie), are not significant. Duluth, South Shore & Atlantic is given a run once or twice a year by the Canadian Pacific following having its headquarters in Montreal.

The Guggenheims are always active in Smelters, and the stock frequently offers splendid trading opportunities. Lead is frequently used as a "chaser," and is often made active when Smelters has completed its rim.

New Haven is mainly held by New Englanders for investment. Ontario & Western is popular with small traders; its movements deserve little consideration.

The Public

U. S. Steel is swayed by conditions in the steel trade, and the speculative temper of the general public, assisted occasionally by some of the insiders. No other stock on the list is such a true index of the attitude of the public, or the technical position of the market. Including those who own the stock outright, and those who carry it on margin, probably a quarter of a million people here and abroad closely follow its movements. Weekly reports of the steel trade are most carefully scrutinized, and the corporation's earnings and orders on hand minutely studied by thousands.

This great public never sells its favorite short, but carries it "paid for," or on margin until a profit is secured, or until it is shaken or scared out in a violent decline. Hence, if the stock is strong under adverse news, we may infer that public holdings are strongly fortified, and that confidence abounds. If Steel displays more than its share of weakness, an untenable position of the public is indicated.

The other steel stocks are dominated by the giant corporation, and seldom furnish indications of value to the Tape Readers, except at the end of a long rise.

At this point public sentiment be comes intensely bullish and spreads itself in the low-priced speculative shares. Insiders in the junior steel stocks take. advantage of this and are able to advance and find a good market for their holdings.

Equipment Stocks

The Equipment Stocks find their chief inspiration in the orders for cars locomotives, etc., placed by the rail roads. These orders are dependent upon general business conditions. Consequently the equipment issues can seldom be expected to do more than follow the trend of prosperity or de pression.

We have thus introduced ourselves to the principal speculative mediums and their families, each of which, upon closer acquaintance, seems to have a sort of personality; If we stand in a room with fifty or a hundred people, all of whom we know, as regards their chief motives and characteristics, we can form definite ideas as to their probable actions under a given set of circumstances. This would be impossible among strangers.

Knowledge of Details

So it becomes the Tape Reader to acquaint himself with the most minute details pertaining to these market identities, also with the habits, motives and methods of the men who make the principal moves on the Stock Exchange chess-board.

IV.
STOP ORDERS, TRADING RULES, &C.

WHEN a person contemplates an extensive trip, one of the first things taken into account is the expense - that. which cannot be avoided. In planning our excursion into the realms of Tape Reading we must, therefore, carefully weigh the expenses, or, to use a better term, the fixed charges in trading.

Expenses

Were there no expenses, profit-making would be far easier - profits would merely have to exceed losses. But no matter whether you are a member of the New York Stock Exchange or not, in actual trading profits must exceed losses *and expenses.* These are incurred in every trade, whether it shows a gain or a loss. They consist of:

Commission on 100 shares	$25.00
Invisible eighth (see TIÇKER, Vol. I, No. 2, p. 17).............	12.50
Tax on sale	2.00
	$39.50

in addition to interest if the trade is carried over night.

By purchasing a New York Stock Exchange seat, the commission can be reduced to $1 per hundred shares, bought and sold the same day, or $3.12½ if carried over night. This advantage is partly offset by interest on the money involved, dues, assessments, etc., which amount to nearly $5,000 per annum on a seat costing $75,000.

The Invisible Eighth

The invisible eighth is a factor which no one - not even a member - can overcome. Nor can the tax be legitimately avoided.

The Tape Reader who is a nonmember must, therefore, realize that *the instant he gives an order* to go long or short 100 shares, *he has lost* $39.50. in order that he may not fool himself, he should add his commissions (¼%) to his purchase price, or deduct them from his selling price *immediately*. People who boast of their profits usually forget to deduct expenses. Yet it is this insidious item which frequently throws the net result over to the debit side.

The expression is frequently heard, "I got out even, except the commissions," the speaker evidently scorning such a trifling consideration. This sort of self-deception is ruinous, as will be seen by computing the fixed charges on 10 trades - $395 - or on 20 trades - $790. Bear in mind that a loss of $39.50 on the first trade leaves double that amount - $79 - to be made on the second trade before a dollar of profit is secured.

Use of Stop Orders

It therefore appears that the Tape Reader's problem is not only to eliminate losses, but to cover his expenses as quickly as may be. If he has a couple of points profit in a long trade, there is no reason why he should let the stock run back below his net buying price. Here circumstances seem to call for a stop order, so that no matter what happens, he will not be compelled to pay out money. This stop should not be thrust in when net cost is too close to the market price. Reactions must be allowed for.

A Tape Reader is essentially one who follows the immediate trend. An expert can readily distinguish between a change of trend and a reaction. When his mental barometer indicates a change he does not wait for a stop order to be caught, but cleans house or reverses his position in a twinkling. The stop order at net cost is, therefore, of advantage only in case of a reversal which is sudden, pronounced, and with no forewarning.

A stop should also be placed if the operator is obliged to leave the tape for more than a moment, or if the ticker gets out of order. While he has his eye on the tape the market will tell him what to do. The moment this condition does not exist he must act as he would if temporarily stricken blind - he must protect himself from forces which may assail him in the dark.

I know a trader who once bought 500 shares of Sugar and then went out to lunch. He paid 25 cents for what he ate, but on returning to the tape he found the total cost of that lunch was $5,000.25. He had left no stop order, Sugar was down ten points, and his broker wore a MM (more margin button) in his lapel.

Accidents

The ticker has a habit of becoming incoherent at the most critical points. Curse it as he may, it will resume printing intelligibly when the trouble is overcome - not before. As the loss of even a few inches of quotations may be important, a stop should be placed at once and left in until the flow of prices is resumed.

If a trade is carried over night, a stop should be entered against the possibility of accident to the market or the trader. An important event may develop before the next day's opening by which the stock will be violently affected. The trader may be taken ill, be delayed in arrival, or in some way become incapacitated. A certain allowance must be made for accidents of every kind.

As to where the stop should be placed under such conditions, this depends upon circumstances. The consensus of shrewd and experienced traders is in favor of two points maximum gross loss on any one trade. This is purely arbitrary, however. The Tape Reader knows, as a rule, what to do when he is at the tape, but if he is separated from the market by any contingency, he will be obliged to fall back upon the arbitrary stop.

Points of Resistance

A closer stop may be obtained by noting the "points of resistance" - the levels at which the market turns after a reaction. For example, if you are short at 130 and the stock breaks to 128, rallies to 129, and then turns down again, the point of resistance is 129. In case of temporary absence or interruption to the service, a good stop would be 129⅛ or 129¼. These "points of resistance" will be more fully discussed later.

Automatic Stops

If the operator wishes to use an automatic stop, a very good method is this: Suppose the initial trade is made with a one-point stop. For every 1/8 the stock moves in your favor, change the stop to correspond, so that the stop is never more nor less than one point away from the extreme market price. This gradually and automatically reduces the risk. and if the Tape Reader be at all skilful, his profits must exceed losses. As soon as the stop is thus raised to cover commissions, it would seem best not to make it automatic thereafter, but let the market develop its own stop or signal to get out.

One trouble with this kind of a stop is that it interferes with the free play of judgment. A homely illustration will explain why: A tall woman and a short man attempt to cross a street. An automobile approaches. The woman sees that there is ample time in which to cross, but he has her by the arm and being undecided himself, backs and fills, first pushing, then pulling her by the arm until they finally return to the curb, after a hairbreadth escape. Left to herself, she would have known exactly what to do.

Uncertainty

It is the same with the Tape Reader. He is hampered by an automatic stop. It is best that he be free to act as his judgment dictates, without feeling compelled by a prior resolution to act according to a hard and fast rule. There is another time when the stop order is of value to the Tape Reader, viz., when his indications are not clearly defined. The original commitment should, of course, be made only when the trend is positively indicated, but situations will develop when he will be uncertain whether to stand pat, close out, or reverse his position. At such a time it seems better to push the stop up to a point as close as possible to the market price, without choking off the trade. By this we mean a reasonable area should be allowed for temporary fluctuations. If the stock emerges from its uncertainty by going in the desired direction, the stop can be changed or cancelled. If its trend becomes adverse, the trade is automatically closed.

Fear

Fear, hesitation and uncertainty are deadly enemies of the Tape Reader. The chief cause of fear is over-trading. Therefore commitments should be no greater than can be borne by one's susceptibility in this respect.

Hesitation

Hesitation must be overcome by self training. To observe a positive indication and not act upon it is fatal - more so in closing than in opening a trade. The appearance of a definite indication should be immediately followed by an order. Seconds are often more valuable than minutes. The Tape Reader is not the captain - he is but the engineer who controls the machinery. The Tape is the pilot and the engineer must obey orders with promptness and precision.

Uncertainty may be reduced by the use of stops as above, or by closing a trade whenever one's course is not entirely clear.

We have defined a Tape Reader as one who follows the immediate trend. This means that he pursues the line of least resistance. He goes *with* the market - he does not buck it. The operator who opposes the immediate trend pits his judgment and his hundred or more shares against the world's supply or demand and the weight of its millions of shares. Armed with a broom, he is trying to stay the incoming tide.

When he goes *with* the trend, the forces of supply, demand and manipulation are working for and with him.

Quiet Markets

A market which swings within a radius of a couple of points cannot be said to have a trend, and is a good one for the Tape Reader to avoid. The reason is: Unless he catches the extremes of the little swings, he cannot pay commissions, take occasional losses and come out ahead. No yacht can win in a dead calm. As it costs him nearly half a point to trade, each risk should contain a probable two to five points profit, or it is not justified.

A mechanical engineer, given the weight of an object, the force of the blow which strikes it, and the element through which it must pass, can figure approximately how far the object will be driven. So the Tape Reader, by gauging the impetus or the energy with which a stock starts and sustains a movement, decides whether it is likely to travel far enough to warrant his going with it – whether it will pay its expenses and remunerate him for his boldness.

The ordinary tip-trading speculator gulps a point or two profit and disdains a loss, unless it is big enough to strangle him. The Tape Reader must do the opposite – he must cut out every possible eighth loss and search for chances to make three, five and ten. points. He does not have to grasp everything that looks like an opportunity. It is not necessary for him to be in the market continuously. He chooses only the best of what the tape offers.

Mental Stops

His original risks can be gradually effaced by clever arrangement of stop orders when a stock goes his way. He may keep these in his head or put them on the floor. For my own part I prefer, having decided upon a danger point, to maintain a mental stop and when the price is reached close the trade at the market. Reason: There may be ground for a change of plan or opinion at the last moment; if a stop is on the floor it takes time to cancel or change it, hence there is a period of a few minutes when the operator does not know where he stands. By using mental stops and market orders he always knows where he stands, except as regards the prices at which his orders are executed. The main consideration is, he knows whether he is in or out.

The placing of stops is most effectual and scientific when indicated by the market itself. An example of this is as follows:

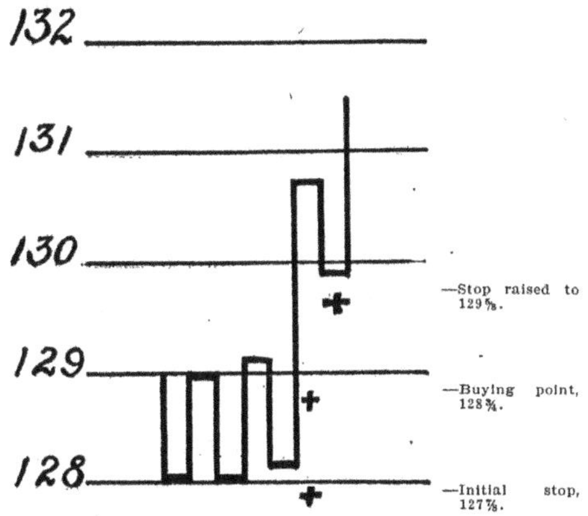

Here a stock, fluctuating between 128 and 129, gives a buying indication at 128¾. Obviously, if the indication is true, the price will not again break 128, having met buying sufficiently strong to turn it up twice from that figure and a third time from 128⅛. The fact that it did not touch 128 on the last down swing forecasts a higher up swing; it shows that the downward pressure was not so strong and the demand slightly more urgent. In other words, the point of resistance was raised ⅛. Having bought .at 128¾, the stop is placed at 127⅞, which is ¼ below the last point of resistance.

Market Indication of Stops

The stock goes above its previous top (129⅛) and continues to 130¾ At any time after it has crossed 130 the operator may raise his stop to cost plus commission (129). The stock reacts at 129⅞, then continues the advance to above 131. As soon as a new high point is reached the stop is raised to 129⅝, as 129⅞ was the point of resistance on the dip.

In such a case the initial risk was ⅞ plus commissions, etc., the market giving a well defined stop point, making an arbitrary stop not only unnecessary but expensive. The illustration is given in chart form, but the experienced Tape Reader generally carries these swings in his head. A series of higher tops and bottoms are made in a pronounced up swing and the reverse in a down swing.

Arbitrary stops may, of course, be used at any time, especially if one wishes to clinch a substantial profit, but until a stock gets away from the price at which it was entered, it seems best to use the stops it develops for itself.

If the operator is shaken out of his holdings immediately after entering the trade, it does not prove his judgment in error. Some accident may have happened, some untoward development in a particular issue, of sufficient weight to affect the rest of the list. It is these unknown quantities that make the limitation of losses most important. In such a case it would be folly to change the stop so that the risk is increased. This, while customary with the public, is something a Tape Reader seldom does. Each trade is made on its own basis, and for certain definite reasons. At the outset the amount of risk should be decided upon, and, except in very rare instances, should not be changed, except on the side of profit. The Tape Reader must eliminate, not enhance, his risk.

No Increase of Risk

Averaging does not come within the province of the Tape Reader. Averaging is groping for the top or bottom. The Tape Reader must not grope. He must see and know, or he should not act.

It is impossible to fix a rule governing the amount of profit the operator should accept. In a general way, there should be no limit set as to the profits. A deal, when entered, may look as though it would yield three or four points, but if the strength increases with the advance it may run ten points before there is any sign of a halt.

We wish our readers to bear fully in mind that these recommendations and suggestions are not to be considered final or inflexible. It is not our aim to assume the role of an oracle. Rather, we are reasoning things out on paper, and as we progress in these studies and apply these tentative rules to the tape, in actual or paper trading, we shall probably have occasion to modify some of our conclusions.

Closing Trades

A Tape Reader must close a trade (1) when the tape tells him to close; (2) when his stop is caught; (3) when his position is not clear; (4) when he has a large or satisfactory profit.

The first and most important reason for closing a trade is: The tape says so. This indication may appear in various forms. Assuming that one is trading in a leader like Union Pacific or Reading, the warning may come in the stock itself. Within the ribbon of sales recorded on the tape, there runs the fine silken thread of the trend. It is clearly distinguishable to one sufficiently versed in the art of Tape Reading, and, for reasons previously explained, is most readily observed in the leaders. Hence when one is short of Union Pacific and this thread suddenly indicates that the market has turned upward, it is folly to remain short. Not only must one cover quickly, but if the power of the movement is sufficient to warrant the risk, the operator must go long. In a market of sufficient breadth and swing, the Tape Reader will find that when it is time to close a trade, it is usually time to reverse his position. One must have the flexibility of whalebone, and entertain no rigid opinion. He must obey the tape implicitly.

Obey the Tape

The indication to close a trade may come from another stock, several stocks or the general market. For example, on January 4th this year, the day of the Supreme Court decision in Consolidated Gas, suppose the operator was long of Union Pacific at 11 o'clock, having paid therefor 182¾.

Large Volumes

Between 11 and 12 o'clock Union rallied to 183½, and Reading, which was more active, to 144. Just before, and immediately after, the noon hour, tremendous transactions took place in Reading, over 50,000 shares changing hands within three-quarters of a point. These may have been largely wash sales, accompanied by inside selling; it is impossible to tell. If they were not, the inference is that considerable buying power developed in Reading at this level and was met by selling heavy enough to supply all bidders and prevent the stock advancing above 144⅜. Large quantities coming within a small range indicated either one of two things: (1) That considerable buying power suddenly developed at this point, and the insiders chose to check it or to take advantage of the opportunity to unload. (2) The demonstration in Reading may have been intended to distract attention from other stocks in which large operators were unloading. (There is no special evidence of this, except in New York Central.)

A Check to Reading

If the selling is not sufficient to check the upward move, the market for Reading will absorb all that is offered and advance, now or later, to a higher level, but in this case the selling was more effectual than the buying, and Reading fell back, warning the operator that the temporary leader on the bull side of the market had met with defeat.

If a stock or the whole market cannot be advanced, the assumption is that it will decline - a market seldom stands still. At this point the operator was; therefore, on the lookout for a slump.

Reading subsided, in small lots, back to 143⅞. Union Pacific, after selling at 183⅝, declined to 183¼. Both stocks developed dullness, and the whole market became more or less without feature.

Suddenly Union Pacific came 183⅛. 500.183.200.182⅞.500.¾, indicating not only a lack of demand, but remarkably poor support. Immediately following this, New York Central, which sold only a few minutes before 400.-131½ came 131.1700.130¼.500.130. This demonstrated that the market was remarkably hollow and in a position to develop great weakness. The large quantities of New York Central at the low figure, after a running decline of a point and one-half, showed that there was not only an absence of supporting orders, but that sellers were obliged to make great concessions in order to dispose of their holdings. The quantities, especially in view of the narrowness of the market, proved that the sellers were not small fry.

Catching the Cue

Coupled with the wet blanket put on Reading and the poor support in Union Pacific, this weakness in New York Central was another advance notice of a decline. On any further indication he must be ready to jump out of his long stock and get short of the market.

Public Buying

While waiting for his cue, the Tape Reader has time to consider which stock among the leaders is the most desirable for selling. He quickly chooses Reading, on the ground that - the large lots which have apparently been distributed around 144 will probably come into the market as soon as weakness develops. Reason: The outside public generally buys on just such bulges as the one which has taken place in Reading. A large volume, even if accompanied by only a fractional advance, has the effect of making the ordinary trader intensely bullish, the result being that he bites off a lot. of long stock at the top of the bulge. This is exactly what the manipulator wishes him to do. We have all heard people boast that their purchase was at the top eighth and that it had the effect of turning the stock down. Those who make their purchases after this fashion are quickest to become scared at the first appearance of weakness, and throw overboard what they have bought. In choosing Reading, therefore, the Tape Reader is picking out the stock in which he is likely to have the most help on the bear side.

Buying at the Top

At 12.30 the market is standing still, the majority of transactions being in small lots and at only fractional changes. Reading shows the effect of the recent unloading. It is coming out 500.143¾.500.⅝.400.½.¾. The operator realizes that Reading is probably a short sale right here, with a stop order at 144½ or ⅝, on the ground that the bulls must have an extraordinary amount of latent buying power in order to push the stock above its former top, where, at every eighth advance over 144⅜, they will encounter a considerable portion of 50,000 shares. This reasoning, however, is all aside from our main argument, which is to show how the cue to get out will be given by stocks other than that in which the operator is working.

Union Pacific shows on the tape in small lots at 182¾; New York Central 1100.130.900.⅜. The rest of the market seems to have all the snap and ginger taken out of it and the operator does not like his position on the long side. He has no definite indication to sell short, however, but feeling that his chances on the long side have been reduced to practically nil by the weak undertone of the market, he therefore gets out of his Union Pacific and waits until the tape tells him to sell Reading short.

Closing Out

Union Pacific weakens to 182⅝. The others slide off fractionally. The weakness is not positive enough to forecast any big break, so he continues to wait. There are 1800 shares of Union altogether at 182⅝, followed by 3000 at 182½. Other stocks respond and the market looks more bearish.

Consolidated Gas comes 163¾.¼. 163. This is the first sign of activity in the stock, but the move is nothing unusual for Gas, as its fluctuations are generally wide and erratic. The balance of the list rallies a fraction. Gas comes 162½.¾.500.162¼. At this point Gas, which has been very dull heretofore, now forces itself, by its decline and weakness, upon the notice of the operator. He begins to look upon the stock as the possible shears which will cut the thread of the market and let everything down.

Break in Gas

12.45 - Gas 500.161½ . It is very weak. The balance of the list is steady, Union Pacific 182⅝, Central 130⅜, Reading 143¾. There is a fractional rally - Union Pacific to 182⅞ and Gas to 162. Plenty of Central for sale around 130; Reading is 143½.

The rally peters out. There is a gradual weakening all around, but the Tape Reader cannot go with the trend until he is sure of a big swing. Central comes 129¾, showing that after all the buyers at 130 are filled up considerable stock is still for sale. The others show only in small lots. The market is on the verge of a decline; it is where a push or a jar of any sort will start it down. Union Pacific is heavy at 182½.300.⅜.200.½, Reading 143½.⅜.1000½, Central 2000.130.800.⅛.

The Thrust

Here is the thrust he has been looking for! Gas 163¾.200.½.400.161.300. 160½.400.160! He waits no longer, but gives an order to sell Reading short at the market. They are all on the run now, Reading 143%.600.%. 1300.%. Central 130.129%, Gas 500, 159%. Something very rotten about Gas and it's a cinch to sell it short if you don't mind trading in a buzz-saw stock. '

The market breaks so rapidly that he does not get over 142¾ for his Reading, but he is short not far from the top of what looks like a wide open break.

Everything is slumping now - Steel, Smelters, Southern Pacific, St. Paul. Union Pacific is down to 181⅝, and the rest in proportion.

The Break

Gas 158½.158.300.157.156.155.154.153 and the rest "come tumbling, after." Reading 141⅜.500.¼.400.141. 140¾.500.½.200.140.600.139¾.500.⅝. Union 181.180⅞.¾.½.¼.600.⅛.500. 180.179¾.500.½.300.¼, Central 127½.

The Break

The above illustrates some of the workings of a Tape Reader's mind ; also how a break in a stock, entirely foreign to that which is being traded in, will furnish the indication to get out and go short of one stock or another.

The indication to close a trade may come from the general market where the trend is clearly developed throughout the list, all stocks working in complete harmony. One of the best indications in this line is the strength or weakness on rallies and reactions. These will be discussed in a subsequent issue.

News From the Tape

Of course the break in Gas, which finally touched 138, is due to the Supreme Court decision, which was announced on the news tickers at 1.1 p. m., but, as is usually the case', the tape told the news many mintues before anything else. This is one of the advantages of getting your news from the first place where it is reflected. Other people who wait for such information to sift through telephone and telegraph wires and reach them by the roundabout way of news tickers or word of mouth, are working under a tremendous handicap.

That not even the insiders knew what the decision was to be is shown in the dullness of the stock- all morning. Those who heard the decision in the Supreme Court chamber doubtless did the double-quick to the telephone and sold the stock short. Their sales showed on the tape before the news arrived in New York. Tape Readers were, therefore, first to be notified. They were short before the Street knew what had happened.

V.
VOLUMES AND THEIR SIGNIFICANCE

AS the whole object of these studies is to learn to read what the tape says, I will now explain a point which is probably one of the most valuable in the practice of the art. This must be known and understood before we proceed, otherwise the explanations cannot be made clear.

"Market Price" Defined

First of all, we must recognize that the market for any stock - at whatever level it may be - is composed of two sides, represented by the bid and the asked price. Please remember that the last sale is something entirely different from the market price. If Steel has just sold at 50, this figure represents what *has* happened. It is history. The *market price* of Steel is either 49⅛@50 or 50@50⅛. *The bid and asked prices combined form the market price.*

This market price is like. a pair of scales, and the volume of stock thrown by sellers and reached for by purchasers shows toward which side the preponderance of weight has momentarily shifted. For example, when the tape shows

US.
500 . 50 . 1000 . ⅛ . 50 . 1500 . ⅛

the market price is 5o@⅛, and the large volumes are on the up side. In these four transactions there are 700 shares sold at 50 against 2,500 taken at 50%, proving that *at the moment* the buying is more urgent than the selling. The deduction here to be made is that Steel will probably sell at 50¼ before 49⅞. There is no certainty in this, for supply and demand is changing with every second, not only in Steel but in every other stock on the list.

Advantage of the Leaders

Here is one advantage in trading in the leaders. The influence of demand or pressure is concentrated or at least strongly felt in the principal stocks. The hand of the dominant power, whether it be an insider, an outside manipulator or the public, is shown in these volumes. Especially is this true in the pivotal stocks, like Union Pacific, Reading and others, which are generally used by the Harriman and Rockefeller parties. The reason is simple. These big fellows cannot put their stocks up or down without trading in enormous amounts. In an advancing market they are obliged to reach up for or bid up their stocks, as, for example:

U
182 . 1000 . ⅛ . 200 . 182 . 1500 . ⅛

200¼ . 3500. ⅜ . 2000 .½ .

In a case like the following, Union Pacific is being bought on a decline whenever round lots come into the market:

Examples

U
200 . 181¼ . 2600 . ⅝ . ½ . 200 .

⅜ . ¼ . ⅛ . 4000 . ¼ . 1500 . ⅜ .

Take the opening and subsequent transactions in American Locomotive one day last fall:

200...47¼	100...45⅞	100... 45%
1900...46¾	100...46⅛	100...46
100...46%	100...46	600...45⅞
100...46½	200...46¼	500...45¾
100...46⅜	100...46⅜	200...45⅝
600...46¼	11 A. M.	100.. .45½

100... 46⅛	300...46⅜	100...45⅝
600...46	100...46⅛	400...45⅞
100...45⅞	100...46	100...45¾
200...45¾	100...45⅞	400...45⅝
100...46	100...46	100...45¾

Here the opening market price was 46¾ @ 47¼, and the buyers of 200 shares "at the market" paid the high price. All bids at 46¾ were then filled. This is proved by the next sale, which is at 46⅝. The big lots thereafter are mostly on the down side, showing that pressure still existed. The indications were, therefore, that the stock would go lower. A lot of 1900 shares in a stock like Locomotive is a large lot; in Union Pacific it would be of frequent occurrence, even in comparatively dull markets.

Proportional Volumes

Volumes must be valued in proportion to the activity of the market, as well as the relative activity of that particular issue. No set rule can be established. I have seen a Tape Reader make money by following the lead of a 1000-share lot of Northwest which someone took at a fraction above the last sale. Ordinarily Northwest is a sluggish investment stock, and this size lot appeared as the forerunner of an active speculative demand.

Now let us see what happens on the floor to produce the above-described effect on the tape - let us prove that our theory is correct. A few years ago the control of a certain railroad was being bought on the floor of the New York Stock Exchange. One house was given all the orders, with instructions to distribute them and conceal the buying as much as possible. The original order for the day would read, "Take everything that is offered up to 38." As 38 was about 3 points above the market of, the day before, this left considerable leeway for the broker to whom the buying order was entrusted.

He would instruct his floor broker as follows: "The stock closed last night at 35. You take everything offered up to 35½ and then report to me how things stand. Don't bid for the stock; just take it as it is offered and mark it down whenever you can."

On the Floor

In such a case the floor member stands in the crowd awaiting the opening. On the instant of ten o'clock the chairman's gavel strikes and the crowd begins yelling. Someone offers "2000 at an eighth." Another broker says "Five for five hundred." Our broker takes the 2000 at ⅛, then offers it at ⅛ himself, so as to keep the price down. Others then offer one or two hundred shares at ⅛, so he withdraws his offer, as he wishes to accumulate and only offers or sells when it helps him buy more, or puts the price down. The buyer at 35 has 300 shares of his lot cancelled, so he alters his. bid to "35 for two hundred." The other sellers supply him and he then bids "⅞ for a hundred." Our broker sells him 100 at ⅞ just to get the market down. Someone comes in with "a thousand at five." Our broker says, "I'll take it." Five hundred more is offered at ⅛. This he also takes.

Let us see how the tape records these transactions:

2000 . 35⅛ . 200 . 35 . 34⅞

. 1000 . 35 . 500 . ⅛

The Tape Reader interprets this: Opening bid and asked price was probably 35@⅛; someone took the large lot at the high price. The two sales following were in small lots, showing light pressure. The 1000@35 after 34⅞. shows that on the ⅞@5 market the buyer took the stock at the offered price and followed it up by taking 500 more at the eighth. The weight is on the up side and it does not matter whether the buyer is one individual or a dozen, the momentary trend is upward.

Marking Down

To get the opposite side, let us suppose a manipulator is desirous of depressing a stock. This can be accomplished by offering and selling more than there is a demand for, or by coaxing or frightening other holders into throwing over their shares. It makes no difference whose stock is sold; "The Lord is on the side of the heaviest battalions," as Addison _ Cammock used to say. When à manipulator puts a broker into a crowd with orders to mark it down, the broker supplies all bids and then offers it down to the objective point or until he meets resistance too strong for him to overcome without the loss of a large block of stock.

The issue in question is selling around 80, we will say, and the broker's orders are to "put it to 77." Going into the crowd, he finds 500 wanted at 79⅞ and 300 offered at 80. Last sale, 100 at 80.

How It is Done

"I'll sell you that five hundred at seven-eighths. A thousand or any part at three-quarters" he shouts.

"I'll take two hundred at three-quarters," says another broker.

"A half for five hundred" yells a voice. "Sold!" is the response. "A half for five hundred more." "Sold!" "That's a thousand I sold you at a half. Five hundred at three-eighths!"

"I'll take a hundred at three-eighths," comes a voice.

"You're on!" is the reply.

"Quarter for five hundred."

"Sold!" is the quick response.

His pounding of the stock would reveal itself on the tape as follows:

X
80 . 500 . 79⅞ . 200 . ¾

1000 . ½ . ⅜ . 500 . ¼

If he met strong resistance at 79 it would appear on the tape something like this:

X
79⅛ . 1000 . 79 . 500 . 79 . 800 . 79 . 300

. ⅛ 1000 . 79 . 500 . ¼ . ⅜ . 200 . ½

showing that at 79 there was a demand for more than he was willing to supply (there might have been 10,000 shares wanted at 79).

Resistance

Frequently a broker meeting such an obstacle will leave the crowd long enough to 'phone his principal. His departure opens the way for a rally, as the stock is no longer under pressure, and the large buying order at 79 is something for floor traders to fall back on. So those in the crowd bid it up to ½ in hopes of scalping a fraction on the long side.

Take another case where two brokers are put into the crowd - one to depress the stock and the other to accumulate it. They play into each other's hands, and the tape makes the following report of what happens:

X
80⅛ . 80 . 200 . 79⅞ . ¾ . 1000 . ⅞

¾ 200 . ⅝ . 500 . ¾ . 300 . ¾ . ½ .

⅜ . 1500 . ½ . ⅜ . 500 . ¼ . ⅛ .

Were we on the floor we should see one broker offering the stock down, while the other grabbed every round lot that appeared. We cannot tell how far down the stock will be put, but when these indications appear it makes us watch closely for the turning point, which is our time to buy.

So far as the Tape Reader is concerned, he does not care whether the move is made by a manipulator, a group of floor traders, the public or a combination of all.

The figures on the tape represent the consensus of opinion, the effect of manipulation and the supply and demand, all combined into concrete units. That is why tape indications are more reliable than what anyone hears, knows or thinks.

A Pair of Scales

With this idea of the pair of scales clearly implanted in our minds, we scan the tape, mentally weighing the leaders in our effort to learn on which side the tendency is strongest. Not a detail must escape our notice. A sudden demand or a burst of liquidation may enable us to form a new plan, revise an old one or bid us wait.

These volume indications are not always clear. Nor are they infallible. It does not do to rely upon the indications of any one stock to the exclusion of the rest. There was a time, in September, 1908, when certain stocks (Union and Reading, if memory is correct) were being rushed up, while the volume indications in the other active stocks showed clearly that they were being distributed as fast as the market would take them. This happens very frequently on a large or small scale. Especially is it apparent at the turning point of a big swing where accumulation or distribution requires some days to complete.

Study of Volumes

Volumes can be studied from the reports printed in the New York *Evening Sun* or the *Wall Street Journal,* but the real way to study them is from the tape. If one is unable to spend five hours a day at the tape while the ticker is in operation, he can arrange with one of the boys in his broker's office to wind the tape up each day and save it for him. This is done most expeditiously by using an automatic reel, which can be had at any store where telegraph instruments are sold. The tape can then be taken home and studied at leisure. A second reel in the study makes it easy to unwind, after which, the tape can be made to run across one's desk just as though it were coming from the ticker.

In studying under these conditions do not let yourself be deceived as to your ability to make money on paper. Imaginary trades prove nothing in Tape Reading. The way to test your powers is to get into the game. Let it be on as small a scale as you like, but make actual trades with real money.

Poor Response

There are times when the foregoing rule of volumes indicates almost the reverse of what we have explained. One of these instances was described in our last chapter. In this case the transactions in Reading suddenly, swelled out of all proportion to the rest of the market and its own previous volume. Notwithstanding the predominance of apparent demand, the resistance offered (whether legitimate or artificial) became too great for the stock to overcome, and it fell back from 144⅜. On the way up these volumes alone suggested a purchase, but the tape showed abnormal transactions accompanied by poor response from the rest of the list. This suggested manipulation and warned the operator to be cautious on the bull side. The volume in Reading was sustained even after the stock reacted, but the large lots were evidently thrown over at the bid prices. On the way up the volumes were nearly all on the up side and the small lots on the. down side. After 144⅜ was reached the large lots were on the down side and the small lots on the up.

The Small Lots

It is just as important to study the small as the large lots. The smaller quantities are like the feathers on an arrow – they indicate that the business part of the arrow is at the other end. In other words, the smaller lots keep one constantly informed as to what fraction forms the other side of the market. To illustrate: During the first five trades in

700...143⅝
500...143¾
5000...143⅝
1700...143¾
200...143⅝
4300...143¾
3700...143⅞
100...144
12 M.
5000...144
1300...143⅞
3000...144
5000...144⅛
2100...144¼
2200...144⅛
3500...144¼
4000...144⅜
3000...144¼
2500...144⅛
3500...144
400...144⅛
1000...144
500...144⅛

```
1100...144
2000...143⅞
2500...143¾
1000...143⅝
```

Turning point in Reading, morning of Jan. 4, 1909 – the day of the Consolidated Gas collapse

Reading, recorded above, the market quotation is shown to have been 5/8@3/4; it then changed to and again to 7/8@4. On the way down it got to be 4@1/8, and at this level the small lots were particularly valuable in showing the pressure which existed.

Volumes at Turning Points

Stocks like Union and Reading usually make this sort of a turning point on a volume of from 25,000 to 50,000 shares. That is, when they meet with opposition on an advance or a decline it must be in some such quantity in order to stem the tide.

Walk into the hilly country and you will probably find a small rivulet running quietly on its way. The stream is so tiny that you can place your hand in its course and the water will back up. In five minutes, however, it overcomes this resistance by going over or around your hand. You fetch a shovel, pile dirt in its path, pack it down hard and say, "There, I've dammed you." But you haven't at all, for the next day you find your pile of dirt washed away. You bring cartloads of dirt and build a substantial dam, and the flow is finally held in check.

Line of Least Resistance

It is the same with an individual stock or the market. Prices follow the line of least resistance. If Reading is going up someone may throw 10,000 shares in its path without perceptible effect. Another lot of 20,000 shares follows; the stock halts, but finally overcomes the obstacle. The seller gives another order – this time 30,000 shares more are thrown on the market. If there are 30,100 shares wanted at that level, the stock will break through and go higher; if only 29,900 shares are needed to fill all bids, the price will recede because demand has been overcome by supply.

It looks as though something like this happened in Reading on the occasion referred to. Whether or not manipulative orders predominated does not change the aspect of the case. In the final shuffling the weight was on the down side.

Volume Study in Union Pacific, Showing 39,300 Shares Sold from 149¾ to 150, Checking the Rise

200	......147⅞	1400	......147⅞	1100	......148¾
6500	....147½	1500	......147¾	200	......148⅝
	146¾	2000 sld.	...147⅜	600	......148½
100	147	500	......147¾	100	......148⅝
500	......146⅞	200	......147⅝	600	......148½
1200	......146¾	200	......147¾	100	......148⅝
1000	......146⅞	1400	......147⅝	1200	......148½
1000	147	1000	......147¾	100	......148⅝
500	......147⅛	200	......147⅝	1700	......148¾
1000	......147¼	1000	......147½	2400	......148⅝
1000	......147⅜	400	......147⅝	100	......148¾
1000	......147¼	1000	......147½	700	......148⅝
500	......147⅛	600	......147⅝	100	......148¾
800	147	800	......147½	100	......148⅝
600	......146⅞	2100	......147⅝	1100	......148¾
600	147	200	......147¾	1600	......148⅞
400	......147⅛	2800	......147⅞	100	149
1000	......147¼	1400	148	700	......148⅞
1800	......147⅛	400	......147⅞	5700	149
2600	......147¼	2100	148	4400	......149⅛
1100	......147⅜	900	......147⅞	100	149
1500	......147¼	1000	148	1500	......149⅛
2900	......147⅜	1800	......148⅛	2500	149
200	......147¼	700	......148¼	1300	......148⅞
1100	......147⅜	400	......148⅛	1100	149
1200	......147¼	2500	148	1600	......148⅞
1800	......147⅜	1300	......148⅛	1600	......148¾
500	......147½	1200	......148¼	1100	......148⅞
2200	......147⅜	500	......148⅛	600	......148¾
2200	......147½	400	......148¼	300	......148⅝
500	......147⅜	2800	......148⅜	600	......148½
500	......147½	500	......148¼	800	......148⅜
500	......147⅜	1200	......148⅜	500	......148½
3000	......147½	3500	......148¼	1000	......148⅜
700	......147⅜	900	......148⅜	1200	......148¼
400	......147½	300	......148½	500	......148⅜
2400	......147⅝	700	......148⅜	3200	......148¼
200	......147½	100	......148¼	600	......148⅜
1300	......147⅝	400	......148⅜	800	......148¼
1700	......147¾	400	......148¼	100	......148⅛
700	......147⅝	1100	......148⅜	800	......148¼
500	......147¾	200	......148½	900	......148⅜
700	......147⅝	200	......148⅜	1700	......148¼
900	......147½	800	......148¼	2600	......148⅛
200	......147⅝	400	......148⅛	100	......148¼
400	......147½	1300	......148¼	100	......148⅜
100	......147⅝	1500	......148⅛	300	......148¼
100	......147½	11 A. M.		1100	......148⅛
1800	......147⅝			400	148
1000	......147½	300	......148¼	500	......148⅛
700	......147⅜	900	......148⅜		
1300	......147½	2200	......148½	12 M.	
700	......147⅜	1500	......148⅝	100	......148⅛
1000	......147½	1900	......148¾	700	......148¼
800	......147⅝	1700	......148⅞	100	......148⅜

1200	......148¼	400	......148⅜	500	......149⅞
100	......148½	1100	......148½	500	......149¾
100	......148⅜	1600	......148⅝	1500	......149⅞
1100	......148½	2700	......148¾	100	......149¾
100	......148⅜	400	......148⅞	500	......149⅝
100	......148½	100	......148¾	1600	......149¾
200	......148⅝	1200	......148⅞	1100	......149⅞
800	......148¾	600	......148¾	100	......149¾
800	......148½	300	......148⅞	500	......149⅞
2900	......148⅝	3200	149	4400	......149¾
1100	......148½	300	......149⅛	1000	......149⅞
500	......148⅜	3000	......149¼	200	......149¾
300	......148¼	1500	......149⅜	100	......149⅝
800	......148⅜	800	......149¼	1200	......149¾
700	......148½	200	......149⅛	200	......149⅝
100	......148⅝	200sld.	...148⅞	300	......149¾
400	......148½	300	......149⅛	800	......149⅝
100	......148¾	700	......149¼	700	......149½
1600	......148⅝	100	......149⅛	100	......149⅜
1800	......148¾	500	......149¼	1400	......149¼
400	......148⅝			1200	......149⅛
400	......148¾	2 P. M.		800	......149¼
900	......148⅝			1700	......149⅛
100	......148½	400	......149¼	2500	149
		700	......149⅜	100	......149⅛
1 P. M.		4300	......149¼	2300	149
		100	......149⅛	500	......148⅞
800	......148½	1300	......149¼	1400	......148¾
100	......148⅞	1500	......149⅜	1600	149
200	......148¼	600	......149¼	700	......148⅞
100	......148⅜	1700	......149⅜	500	......148¾
100	......148¼	600	......149¼	800	......148⅝
100	......148½	1600	......149⅜	100	......148⅝
600	......148⅜	2800	......149½	400	......148¾
100	......148½	1400	......149⅝	2300	......148⅝
100	......148⅜	500	......149¾	200	......148¾
900	......148¼	600	......149⅝	2800	......148⅝
100	......148⅞	10300	......149¾	1200	......148½
200	......148¼	5800	......149⅞	200	......148⅜
500	......148¼	6000	150	900	......148½
500	......148⅛	1600	......149⅞	1000	......148⅝
100	148	300	150	400	......148½
700	......148⅛	800	......149⅞	500	......148⅝
800	......148¼	1000	......149¾	1500	......148¾

The public and the floor traders do not stand aside while the manipulator is at work, nor is the reverse true. Everybody's stock looks alike on the tape. The ticker plays no favorites.

When a stream breaks through a dam it goes into new territory. Likewise the breaking through of a stock is significant, for it means that the resistance has been overcome. The stronger the resistance the less likelihood of finding further obstacles in the immediate vicinity – dams are not usually built one behind the other. So when we find a stock emerging into a new field it is best to go with it, especially if, in breaking through it, it carries the rest of the market along.

A Live Tape

While much can be learned from the reports printed in the dailies mentioned above, the tape itself is the only real instruction book. A live tape is to be preferred, for the element of speed with which the ticker prints is no small factor. The comparative activity of the market on bulges and breaks is a guide to the technical condition of the market. For "instance, during a decline, if the ticker is very active and the volume of sales large, voluntary or compulsory liquidation is indicated. This is .emphasized if, on the subsequent rally, the tape moves sluggishly and only small lots appear. In an active bull market the ticker appears to be choked with the volume of sales poured through it on the advances, but on reactions the quantities and the number of impressions decrease until, like the ocean at ebb tide, the market is almost lifeless.

Another indication of the power of a movement is found in the differences between sales of active stocks, for example:

```
U
  1000 . 180 . ⅛ . 500 . ⅜ . 1000 . ½
```

Jumps

This shows that there was only 100 shares for sale at 180⅛, none at all at 180%, and only 500 at 180⅜. The jump from ⅛ to ⅜ emphasizes both the absence of pressure and persistency on the part of the buyers. They are not content to wait patiently until they can secure the stock at 180%; they reach for it, and, finding themselves clutching the air, are obliged to reach higher. The same thing on the opposite side shows lack of support.

Each indication is to be judged not so much by rule as according to the conditions surrounding it. The tape furnishes a continuous series of motion pictures, with their respective explanations written between the printings. These are in a language which is foreign to all but Tape Readers, but anyone can learn a foreign language.

Effect of Manipulation

These volumes which we have been discussing are least liable to mislead when manipulation prevails, for the manipulator is obliged to deal in large blocks of stock, and must continually show his hand. A complete manipulative operation on the long side consists of three parts: Accumulation, marking up, and distribution. In the case of a short operation the distribution comes first, then the mark down and the accumulation. No one of these three sections is complete without the other two. (For full details see my series on Manipulations in Vols. 1 and 2 of The Ticker.)

The manipulator must work with a large block of stock or the deal will not be worth his time, the risk and expenses. The Tape Reader must, therefore, be on the lookout for extensive operations on either side of the market. Accumulation will show itself in the quantities and in the way they appear on the tape. Having detected the accumulation, the Tape Reader has only to watch its progress, holding himself in readiness to take on some of the issue the moment the marking-up period begins. He does not buy it at once, because it may take weeks or months for the manipulator to complete his line; also, there might be opportunities to buy cheaper. Holding off until the psychological moment forces someone else to carry the stock for him - to pay his interest, so to speak. Furthermore, his capital is left free in the meantime.

The Psychological Moment.

When the marking up begins he gets in at the commencement of the move, and goes along with it till there are signs of a halt or distribution. Having passed through the first two periods, he is in a position to fully benefit by the third stage of the operation. In this sort of work a figure chart, which I described in Vol 1 of The Ticker, will help him, especially if the manipulative operation is continued over a considerable period - it will give him a bird's-eye view of the deal, enabling him to drop or resume the thread at any stage.

VI.
MARKET TECHNIQUE

ON Saturday morning, February 27th, the market opened slightly higher than the previous night's close. Reading was the most active stock. After touching 123½ it slid off to 122%, at which point it invited short sales. This indication was emphasized at 122, at 121½ and again at 121. The downward trend was strongly marked until it struck 119⅞; then followed a quick rally of 1⅛ points.

Strong Resistance

This was a vicious three-point jab into a market which was only just recovering from the February break. What was its effect on the other principal stocks? Union Pacific declined only ¾, Southern Pacific ⅝ and Steel This proved that they were technically strong; that is, they were in hands which could view with equanimity a three-point break in a leading issue. Had this drive occurred when Reading was around 145 and Union 185 the effect upon the others would probably have been very different.

Floating Supply

In order to determine the extent of an ore body, miners use a diamond drill. This produces a core, the character of which shows what is beneath the surface. If it had been possible to have drilled into the market at the top of the recent rise, we should have found that the bulk of the floating supply in Steel, Reading and some others was held by a class of traders who buy heavily in booms and on bulges. These people operate with a comparatively small supply of margins, nerve and experience. They are exceedingly vulnerable, hence the stocks in which they operate suffer the greatest declines when the market receives a jar. The figures are interesting.

-- Points --		Per cent. of break to adv.
1907-9 Advance.	Feb'y, '09 Break.	
U. P. 84⅞	12⅜	14.7
Reading 73⅞	26⅜	33.6
Steel 36⅞	16½	44.6

The above shows that the public was heavily extended in Steel, somewhat less loaded with Reading, and was carrying very little Union Pacific. In other words, Union showed technical strength by its resistance to pressure, whereas Reading and Steel offered little or no opposition to the decline.

Technical Conditions

Both the market as a whole and individual stocks are to be judged as much by what they do as what they do not do at critical points. If the big fellows who accumulated Union below 120 had distributed it above 180, the stock would have broken something like thirty points, owing to its having passed from strong to weak hands. As it did not have any such decline, but only a very small reaction, compared to its advance, the Tape Reader infers that Union is destined for much higher prices; that it offers comparative immunity from declines and a possible large advance in the near future.

A Three-point Break in Reading which had little effect upon the other leader, proving the market technically strong

Reading Co.					
		2100	......121¾	200	......120⅝
1700	123	300	......121⅝	500	......120⅞
200	......123⅛	2000	......121½	1200	121
500	123	11 A. M.		200	......120⅞
500	......122⅞	1700	......121¼	100	......120¾
1300	123	200	......121⅜	600	......120⅞
500	......123⅛	600	......121¼	1000	121
1900	......123¼	100	......121⅜	700	......121¼
1500	......123⅛	2700	......121¼	400	......121⅛
200	......123¼	100sld.	...121⅛	900	......121¼
400	......123⅛	200	......121⅜	400	......121⅜
1100	123	400	......121¼	700	......121¼
1200	......123⅛	1400	......121½	1000	......121⅛
300	......122⅞	200	......121⅜	600	121
1500	......122¾	400	......121¼	1000	......121¼

1400 ......122⅝
1200 ......122½
100 ......122⅝
3000 ......122½
200 ......122⅜
700 ......122½
100 ......122⅝
2000 ......122⅜
500 ......122½
200 ......122⅜
100 ......122¼
500 122
100 ......122⅛
800 ......122¼
100 ......122⅜
100 ......122½
600 ......122⅜
700 ......122¼
1200 ......122⅛
100 ......122¼
100 ......122⅛
100 ......122¼
100 ......122⅜
2100 ......122¼
400 122
300 ......122⅛
500 ......122¼
200 ......122⅛
1500 122
200 ......122⅛
100 122
1900 ......122⅛
1600 122
100 ......122⅛
500 122
100 ......121⅞
1500 122
300 ......121⅞
500 ......121¾
1500 ......121⅞

1100 121
100 ......120⅞
100 121
700 ......120⅞
1400 ......120⅝
700 ......120½
700 ......120⅝
1400 ......120¾
100 ......120⅝
900 ......120½
2000 ......120¼
100 ......120⅜
500 ......120¼
500 ......120⅜
1500 ......120½
800 ......120⅜
600 ......120¼
400 ......120⅜
300 ......120¼
800 ......120⅛
200 ......120⅜
100 ......120½
1300 ......120⅜
1600 ......120½
600 ......120⅜
700 ......120¼
2000 120
100 ......120⅛
1500 120
100 ......119⅞
200 120
200 ......120⅛
200 120
1000 ......120⅛
1700 ......119⅞
200 120
100 ......119⅞
1600 120
1100 ......120⅛
500 ......120½

1100 ......121⅜
1000 ......121¼
200 ......121⅜
100 ......121½
200 ......121⅝
300 ......121⅜
1200 ......121½
500 ......121⅝
1500 ......121¾
1200 ......121⅞
500 ......121¾
200 ......121⅝
800 ......121½

Un. Pac. Ry.

1500 177
500 ......176⅞
1900 177
700 ......176⅞
700 177
600 ......176⅞
500 177
1500 ......177⅛
1200 ......177¼
1200 ......177⅜
200 ......177¼
600 ......177⅜
300 ......177¼
1100 ......177⅜
900 ......177½
2400 ......177⅜
200 ......177¼
100 ......177⅜
700 ......177¼
500 ......177⅜
1300 ......177¼
200 ......177⅜
1200 ......177¼
1700 ......177⅜
2000 ......177¼
200 ......177⅛

1200 ......177¼
300 ......177⅜
100 ......177½
300 ......177⅜
700 ......177¼
1100 ......177⅜
1600 ......177½
300 ......177⅜
900 ......177¼
100 ......177⅜
100 ......177¼
600 ......177⅛
1300 ......177¼
700 ......177⅛

11 A. M.

100 177
3900 ......177⅛
1200 177
1500 ......176⅞
200 ......176¾
1300 ......176⅞

200 ......117⅜
100 ......117½
1100 ......117⅜
200 ......117¼
300 ......117⅜
400 ......117¼
200 ......117⅛
100 ......117¼
200 ......117⅛
100 ......117⅜
600 ......117¼
20 ......117⅜
600 ......117⅜
100 ......117¼
500 ......117⅛
200 117
100 ......117⅛
400 117
300 ......117⅛
100 117

11 A. M.

9100 ...... 44⅝
2000 ...... 44¾
2700 ...... 44⅝
2500 ...... 44¾
400sld. ... 44½
600 ...... 44¾
700 ...... 44⅝
100 ...... 44¾
200 ...... 44⅝
500 ...... 44¾
100 ...... 44⅝
2000 ...... 44¾
900 ...... 44⅝
100 ...... 44¾
1400 ...... 44⅝
600 ...... 44½
1800 ...... 44⅝
2600 ...... 44½
500 ...... 44⅝
100 ...... 44½
1700 ...... 44⅝
1500 ...... 44½

700	177			900	...... 44⅝
100	......176⅞	300	......116⅞	1400	...... 44½
6300	......176¾	400	117	1600	...... 44⅜
1100	......176⅞	500	......116⅞	2100	...... 44¼
200	177	400	117		
1400	......176⅞	100	......116⅞	11 A. M.	
1600	177	100	......116¾	5600	...... 44¼
100	......176⅞	1400	......116⅞	500sld.	... 44⅜
1300	177	100	......116¾	1900	...... 44¼
200	......177⅛	100	......116⅞	200	...... 44⅛
200	177	100	......116¾	700	...... 44¼
1900	......177⅛	100	......116⅞	100	...... 44⅛
500	......177¼	900	......116¾	1200	...... 44¼
1400	......177⅛	700	......116⅞	1100	...... 44⅛
Southern Pac.		200	......116¾	2500	...... 44¼
500	......117¼	400	......116⅞	2500	...... 44⅛
400	......117⅛	400	117	5000	...... 44¼
200	......117¼	U. S. Steel		3200	...... 44⅜
1800	......117⅜	3000	....{ 44½	500	...... 44½
400	......117¼		{ 44⅝	100	...... 44⅜

This should not be taken as a prediction. Even were Union Pacific scheduled for a thirty-point rise in the next two weeks, something might happen to-morrow to postpone the campaign for a considerable time. But the Tape Reader must work with these broader considerations in full view. He has just so much time and capital and this must be employed where it will yield the greatest results. If by watching for the most favorable opportunities he can operate with the trend in a stock which will some day or week show him ten points profit over any other issue he could have chosen, he is increasing his chances to that extent.

A long advance or decline usually culminates in a wide, quick movement in the leaders. Take the break of February 23d last: Reading declined from 128¾ to 118 and Steel from 46 to 41¼ in one day. Southern Pacific, after creeping up last fall from 97 to 112, reached a climax in a seven-point jump during one session. Instances are so numerous that they are hardly worth citing. The same thing happens in the market as a whole – an exceptionally violent movement, after a protracted sag or rise, usually indicates its culmination.

Culminations

A stock generally shows the Tape Reader what it proposes to do by its action under pressure or stimulation. For example: On Friday,

February 19th, 1909, the United States Steel Corporation announced an open market in steel products. The news was out. Everybody in the country knew it by the following morning. The Tape Reader, in weighing the situation before the next day's opening, would reason: "As the news is public property, the normal thing for Steel and the market to do is to rally. Steel closed last night at 48%. The market hinges upon this one stock. Let's see how it acts."

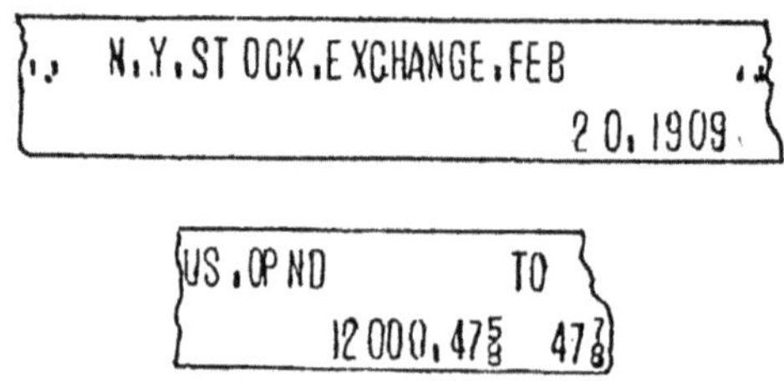

This is ¾ down from last night's closing – a perfectly natural occurrence in view of yesterday's announcement. The real test of strength or weakness will follow. For the first ten minutes Steel comes

200 . 47⅞ . 4500 . ¾ . 1200 . ⅞ . 1500 . ¾

without otherwise varying.

Eighteen times the price swings back and forth between the same fractions. Meantime, Union Pacific, which opened at 177½, show's a tendency to rally and pull the rest of the market up behind it.

U
1200 . 178 . 200 . ⅛ . 400 . ¼ . 200 . 178¼ . 700 . ⅜

An Interesting Contest

Can Union lift Steel? That is the question. Here are two opposing forces, and the Tape Reader watches like a hawk, for he is going with the market – in the direction of the trend. Union is up ⅞ from the opening and Southern Pacific is reinforcing it.

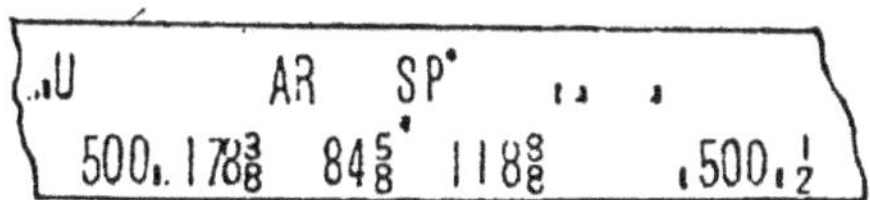

But Steel does not respond. Not once does it get out of that rut – not even a single hundred shares sells at 48. This proves that it is freely offered at 47⅞ and that it possesses no rallying power, in spite of the leadership displayed by the Harrimans.

Union makes a final effort to induce a following,

U
2000.178½

to which Steel replies by breaking through with a thud.

US
800.47⅝.½

The Signal

This is the Tape Reader's cue to go short. In an instant he has put out a line of Steel for which he gets 47½ or 47⅜, as there are large volumes traded in at those figures.

Union Pacific is disheartened. The Steel millstone is hanging round its neck. It slides off to 178¾ . ¼ . ⅛ and finally to

U C CO US
600.178.400.177⅞ 300.73⅛* 66 200.47½

The pressure on Steel increases at the low level.

US NP US
3500.47½ 4S,1,103½ 47⅜

Successive sales are made, as follows:

6800 . 47½ . 2600 . ⅜ . 500¼ . 8800 . ⅛

Liquidation

From this time on there is a steady flow of long stock. Reading and Pennsylvania are the weakest railroads. Colorado Fuel breaks 7 points in a running decline and the other steel stocks follow suit. U. S. Steel is dumped in bunches at the bid prices, and even the dignified preferred is sympathetically affected.

US , PR
500,46⅝ ,3500,½ 200,110¼,200,⅛,1600,110

The market closes at the bottom, with Steel at 46, leaving thousands of stockholders of Steel in a thoroughly frightened state, their accounts weakened by the decline and a holiday ahead for them to worry over.

It looks to the Tape Reader as though the stock would go lower on the following Tuesday. At any rate, no covering indication has appeared, and unless it is his invariable rule to close every trade each day, he puts a stop at 47 on his short Steel and goes his way. (His original stop was 48⅛.)

Steel opens on the following session at 44¾@½, and during the day makes 41¼.

There are a number of lessons to be drawn from this episode. The market is a tug-o'-war. Successful tape reading requires ability to judge which side has the greatest pulling power and one must have the courage to go with that side. There are critical points which occur in each swing, just as in the life of a business or of an individual. At these junctures it seems as though a feather's weight on either side would determine the immediate trend. Any one who can spot these points has everything to win and little to lose, for he can always play with a stop placed close behind the turning point or point of resistance.

Critical Points

If Union had continued in its upward course, gaining in power, volume and influence as it progressed, the dire effects of the Steel situation might have been overcome. It was simply a question of pulling power, and Steel pulled Union down.

Responses

This study of responses is one of the most valuable in the Tape Reader's education. It is an almost unerring guide to the technical position of the market. Of course, all responses are not clearly defined. It is a matter of indifference to the Tape Reader as to who or what produces these tests, or critical periods. They constantly appear and disappear; he must make his diagnosis and act accordingly. If a stock is being manipulated higher, the movement will seldom be continued unless other stocks follow and support the advance. If the public is in control of a stock, the other issues should be watched to see whether large operators are unloading on the strong spots. Should a stock fail to break on bad news. it means that insiders have anticipated the decline and stand ready to buy.

A member of a syndicate once said to me:

"We are going to dissolve to-morrow."

"Will there not be considerable selling by people who don't want to carry their share of the securities?" I asked.

"Well," he replied, "we know how every one stands. Probably 10,000 shares will come on the market from a few members who are obliged to sell, and as a few of us have sold that much short in anticipation, we'll be there to buy it when the time comes."

The Turn in Rock Island

This reminds us that it is well to consider the insider's probable attitude on a stock. The tape usually indicates what this is. One of the muckraking magazines recently showed that Rock Island preferred had been driven down to 28 last August, to the accompaniment of receivership rumors. The writer of the article was unable to prove that these rumors originated with the insiders, but states that the transactions at this time were inscrutable. Perhaps they were inscrutable to a person inexperienced in tape reading, but we well remember that the indications were all in favor of buying the stock; the transactions were very large - out of all proportion to the capital stock outstanding and the floating supply. What did this mean to the Tape Reader? Thousands of shares of stock were traded in per day, after a ten- point decline and a small rally. If the volume of sales represented long stock, some one was there to buy it. If there was manipulation it certainly was not for the purpose of distributing the stock at such a low level. So, by casting out the unlikely factors, we arrived at the correct conclusion. We state this advisedly, because we stood at the ticker and reasoned the situation out at the time.

Floor Traders

The market is being put to the test continually by one element of which little has been said, viz., the floor traders. These shrewd fellows are always on the alert to ferret out a weak spot in the market, for they love the short side. Lack of support, if detected, in an issue generally leads to a raid which if the technical situation is weak spreads to other parts of the floor and produces a reaction or a slump all around. Or, if they find a vulnerable short interest, they are quick to bid up a stock and drive the shorts to cover. With these and other operations going on all the time, the Tape Reader who is at all expert is seldom at a loss to know on which side his best chances lie. Other people are doing for him what he would do himself if he were all-powerful.

The Broad Movements

While it is the smaller swings that interest him most, the Tape Reader must not fail to keep his bearings in relation to the broader movements of the market. When a panic prevails he recognizes in it the birth of a bull market and operates with the certainty that prices will gradually rise until a boom marks the other extreme of the swing. In a bull market he considers reactions of from two to five points normal and reasonable; he looks for occasional drops of 10 to 15 points in the leaders, with a 25-point break at least once a year. When any of these occur, he knows what to look for next.

In a bull market he expects a drop of 10 points to be followed by a recovery of at least half the decline, and if the rise is to continue, all of the drop and . more will be recovered. If a stock or the market refuses to rally naturally, he knows that the trouble has not been overcome, and therefore looks for a further decline.

Take American Smelters, which made a top at 99⅝ last November, then slumped off under rumors of competition until it reached 78. Covering indications appeared around 79½. Had the operator also gone long here, he could confidently have expected Smelters to rally to 88¾. The decline having been 21⅝ points, there was a rally of 10¾ points due. As a matter of record the stock did recover to 89⅜.

Guide Posts

Of course, these things, are mere guide posts, as the Tape Reader's actual trading is done only on the most positive and promising indications; but they are valuable in teaching him what to avoid. For instance, he would be wary about making an initial short sale of Smelters after a 15-point break, even if his indications were clear. There might be several points more on the short side, but he would realize that every point further decline would bring him closer to the turning point, and after such a violent break the safest money was on the long side.

Another instance: Reading sold on January 4th, 1909, at 144⅜. By the end of the month it touched 131½, and on February 23d broke ten points to 118. This was a decline of 24⅜ points, allowing for the 2 per cent. dividend. As previously stated, the stock looked like an attractive short sale, not only on the first breakdown, but on the final drive. The conservative trader would have waited for a buying indication, as there would have been less risk on the long side. The element of safety is as important as any other.

It is seldom that the market runs more than three or four consecutive days in one direction without a reaction, hence the Tape Reader must realize that his chances decrease as the swing is prolonged.

The daily movements offer his best opportunities; but he must keep in stocks which swing wide enough to enable him to grab a profit.

An Hourly Cycle

It is an astonishing fact, and one which we have never before seen in print, that there is a market cycle which runs almost exactly one hour.

Watch it for yourself when next at the ticker, and you will find that if an upward movement culminates at 10:25 the reaction usually will last till 10:55, and the apex of the next up swing will occur about thirty minutes later. I have actually stood watch in hand, having decided what to do, waiting for the high or low moment on which to sell or buy, and have often hit within a fraction of the best obtainable figure. Why this is I do not attempt to explain, but it happens very often.

I have frequently used this idea as a test of the market's strength or weakness, in this way: If a decline ended at a certain moment and the subsequent rally only lasted ten minutes, instead of the normal half hour, I would consider it an indication of weakness and would look for a further decline.

This is valuable more as a check on over-anxiety to act, as it gives a definite point at which commitments may be made to greatest advantage. As Napoleon said: "The adroit man profits by everything, neglects nothing which may increase his chances."

Napoleon's Maxim

I once knew a speculator who bought and sold by the clock. He had no idea of the hourly swing, but would buy at 12 o'clock, because it was 12 o'clock, and would sell at 2 o'clock, for the same reason.

The methods employed by the average outside speculator are not so very much of an improvement on this, which explains why so many lose their money.

The expert Tape Reader is diametrically opposed to such people and their methods.

Science and Skill

He applies science and skill in his angling for profits.

He studies, figures, analyzes and deduces. He knows exactly where he stands, what he is doing and why.

Few people are willing to go to the very bottom of things. Is it any wonder that success is for the few?

VII. DULL MARKETS AND THEIR OPPORTUNITIES

MANY people are apt to regard a dull market as a calamity. They claim: "Our hands are tied; we can't get out of what we've got; if we could there'd be no use getting in again, for whatever we do we can't make a dollar."

Tape Sitters

Such people are not Tape Readers. They are. Sitters. They are Billikens ex-grin.

As a matter of fact, dull markets offer innumerable opportunities and we have only to dig beneath the crust of prejudice to find them.

Dulness in the market or in any special stock means that the forces capable of influencing it in either an upward or a downward direction have temporarily come to a balance. The best illustration is that of a clock which is about run down - its pendulum gradually decreases the width of its swings until it comes to a complete standstill, thus:

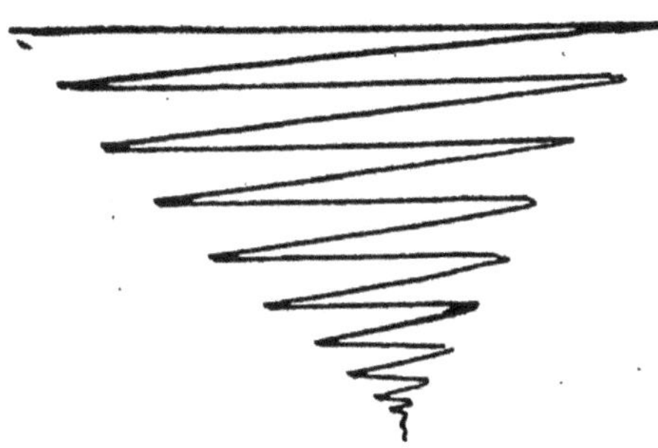

How the market pendulum comes to a standstill

Now turn this on its side and you see what the chart of a stock or the market looks like when it reaches the point of dulness.

These dull periods occur most frequently after a season of delirious activity on the bull side. People make money, pyramid on their profits and glut themselves with stocks at the top. As every one is loaded up, there is comparatively no one left to buy, and the break which inevitably follows would happen if there were no bears, no bad news or anything else to force a decline.

Nature's Remedy

Nature has her own remedy for dissipation. She presents the débauché with a thumping head and a moquette tongue. These tend to keep him quiet until the damage can be repaired.

So with these intervals of market rest. Traders who have placed themselves in a position to be trimmed are duly trimmed. They lose their money and (temporarily) their nerve. The market, therefore, becomes neglected. Extreme dulness sets in.

If the history of the market were to be written, these periods of lifelessness should mark the close of each chapter. The reason is: The factors which were active in producing the main movement, with its start, its climax and its collapse, have spent their force. Prices, therefore, settle into a groove, where they remain sometimes for weeks or until affected by some other powerful influence.

When a market is in the midst of a big move, no one can tell how long or how far it will run. But when prices are stationary, we know that *from this point* there will be a pronounced swing in one direction or another.

The Next Swing

There are ways of anticipating the direction of this swing. One is by noting the technical strength or weakness of the market, as described in a previous chapter. The resistance to pressure men- tionèd as characteristic of the dull period in March, 1909, has been followed by a pronounced rise, and at this writing the leading stocks are many points higher. This is particularly true of Reading, in which the shakeouts around 120 (one of which was described) were frequent and positive. When insiders shake other people out it means that they want the stock themselves. These are good times for us to get in, for then we will enjoy having Mr. Frick and his friends work for *us.*

When a dull market shows its inability to hold rallies, or when it does not respond to bullish news, it is technically weak, and unless something comes along to change the situation, the next swing will be downward.

On the other hand, when there is a gradual hardening in prices; when bear raids fail to dislodge considerable quantities of stock; when stocks do not decline upon unfavorable news, we may look for an advancing market in the near future.

Watch a Dull Market

No one can tell when a dull market will merge into a very active one; therefore the Tape Reader must be constantly on the watch. It is foolish for him to say: "The market is dead dull. No use going downtown to-day. The leaders only swung less than a point yesterday. Nothing in such a market."

Such reasoning is apt to make one miss the very choicest opportunities, viz., those of getting in on the ground floor of a big move. For example: During the aforesaid accumulation in Reading, the stock ranged between 120 and 124%. Without warning, it one day gave indication (around 125) that the absorption was about concluded, and the stock had begun its advance. The Tape Reader, having reasoned beforehand that this accumulation was no piker's game, would have grabbed a bunch of Reading as soon as the indication appeared. He might have bought more than he wanted for scalping purposes, with the intention of holding part of his line for a long swing, using the rest for regular trading.

As the stock drew away from his purchase price he could have raised his stop on the lot he intended to hold, putting a mental label on it to the effect that it is to be sold when he detects inside distribution. Thus he stands to benefit to the fullest extent by any manipulative work which may be done. In other words, he says: "I'll get out of this lot when Mr. Frick and his friends get out of theirs."

Accumulation

He feels easy in his mind about this stock, because he has seen the accumulation and knows it has relieved the market of all the floating supply at about this level.

This means a sharp, quick rise sooner or later, as little stock is to be met with on the way up. If he neglected to watch the market continuously and get in at the very start, his chances would be greatly lessened. He might not have the courage to take on the larger quantity.

On Friday, March 26, 1909, Reading and Union were about as dull as two gentlemanly leaders could well be. Reading opened at 132¾, high was 133¼, low 132%, last 132⅝. Union's extreme fluctuation was ⅝ – from 180⅝ to 181%. Activity was confined to such "pups" as Beet Sugar, Mexican Central and Kansas City Southern.

The following day, Saturday, the opening gave every indication that the previous day's dulness would be repeated, initial sales showing only fractional changes. Copper, B. & O., Wabash pfd. and MOP were up ⅜ or½. Union was ⅛ higher and Reading ⅛ lower. Beet Sugar was down ⅝, with sales at 32.

Reading showed 1100 . 132½ . 800 . ⅜, Union 800 . 181 . 400 . 181 . 200 . . 400 . 181. A single hundred Steel at 45⅛. B. & O. 109⅞ . %. Reading 132%. Beet Sugar 31¾ . 400 . ⅞. Union 800 . 180⅞. Steel 1000 . 45. Beet 800 . 32. Steel 1500 . 45. Reading 132⅝. Steel 44⅞. Market dead. Mostly 100-share lots.

Reading 1600 . 132%. Steel 400.45. Beet Sugar looks good on the bull side, 300.32¼ . 700 . %. Union 200 . 180%. Reading 500 . 132⅜. Union 300 . 180¾.

10.15 A. M. – American Sugar now responds slightly to the strength in Beet Sugar, but we should rather not see. the cart before the horse. Sugar 200 . 130⅞ . 600 . 131. Beet 32½ . 600 . ⅝. This stock holds the spot-light. Others inanimate.

The Cue

Ah! Here's our cue! Reading 2300 • 132½ . 2000 . ½ . 500 . ⅝. Coming out of a dead market, quantities like these taken at the offered prices can mean only one thing, and without quibbling the Tape Reader takes on a bunch of Reading "at the market."

Whatever is doing in Reading, the rest of the market is slow to respond, although N. Y. Central seems willing to help a little – 500 .

127½ (after ¼). Beets are up to 33%. Steel is 45⅛, and Copper 71¼ – a fraction better.

Reading 300 . 132½. Steel 1300 . 45⅛ . ¼. Union 181. Reading 300 . 132⅝. Beets 33½. Union 700 . 181⅛. N. Y. Central 127⅝ . 600 . 54 . ⅞. There's some assistance!

Union 900 . 181⅛. Reading 132¾. Copper 700.71½. Reading 800 . 132⅞. 133 . 900 . 133 . 1100 . ⅛. Central 300 . 127¾. Union 400 . 181⅛ . 300 . ¼. Reading 1500 . 133¼ . 3500 . ½. Not much doubt about the trend now. The whole market is responding to Reading, and there is a steady increase in power, breadth and volume. The rapid advances show that short covering is no small factor. Union 400 . 181⅜ . 700.½.400 . ⅝.

Getting Into Active Stocks

It looks as though a lot of people are throwing their Beet Sugar and getting into the big stocks. St. Paul, Copper and American Smelters begin to lift a little.

Around 11 A. M. there is a brief period of hesitation, in which the market seems to take a long breath in preparation for another effort. There is scarcely any reaction and no weakness. Reading backs up a fraction to 133 ¼ and Union to 181⅜. There are no selling indications, so the Tape Reader stands by his guns.

Now they are picking up again – Reading 133⅜ . ½ . ⅝ . ¾. Union 181⅝. Central 128% . 700 . %. Atchison 1000 . 104% . 600 . ⅝. Northern Pacific is complaisant, 141½ . ⅝. Union 1000 . 181½ . 3500 . ⅝ . 2800 . ¾ . 2800 . ⅞ . 4100 . 182. Steel 45%. Southern Pacific 121. St. Paul 146. Reading 2100 . 133⅞ . 1100 . 134 . 1700 • ⅛.

From then right up to the close it's nothing but bull, and everything closes within a fraction of its highest. Reading makes 134⅜, Union 183, Steel 46⅛, Central 128⅞, and the rest in proportion. The market has gained such headway that it will take dire news to prevent a high, wide opening on Monday, and the Tape Reader has his choice of closing out at the high point or putting in a stop and taking his chances over Sunday.

Breaking Over the Line

So we see the advantage of watching a^ dull market and getting in the moment it starts out of its rut. One could almost draw lines on the chart of a leader like Union or Reading (the upper line being the high point of its monotonous swing and the lower line . the low point) and buy or sell whenever the line is crossed. For when a stock shakes itself loose from a narrow radius it is clear that the accumulation or distribution or resting spell has been completed and new forces are at work. These forces are most pronounced and effective at the beginning of the new move - more power is needed to start a thing rolling than to keep it going.

Some of my readers may think I am giving illustrations after these things happen on the tape, and that what a Tape Reader *would have done* at the time is problematical. I therefore wish to state that my tape illustrations are taken from the indications which actually showed themselves when they were freshly printed on the tape, at which time I did not know what was *going* to happen.

Points of Resistance

There are other ways in which a trader may employ himself during dull periods. One is to keep tab on the points of resistance in the leaders and play on them for fractional profits. This, we admit, is a rather precarious occupation, as the operating expenses constitute an extremely heavy percentage against the player, especially when the leading stocks only swing a point or so per day.

But if one chooses to take these chances rather than be idle, the best way is to keep a chart on which should be recorded every ⅛ fluctuation. This forms a picture of what is occurring and clearly defines the points of resistance, as well as the momentary trend. In the following chart the stock opens at 181¼ and the first point of resistance is 181%. The first indication of a downward trend is shown in the dip to 181⅛, and with these two straws showing the tendency, the Tape Reader goes short "at the market," getting, say, 181⅛ (we'll give ourselves the worst of it).

Tops and Bottoms

After making one more unsuccessful attempt to break through the resistance at 181½, the trend turns unmistakably downward, as shown by an almost unbroken series of lower tops and bottoms. These indicate that the pressure is heavy enough to force the price to new low levels, and at the same time it is sufficient to prevent the rally going quite as high as on the previous bulge.

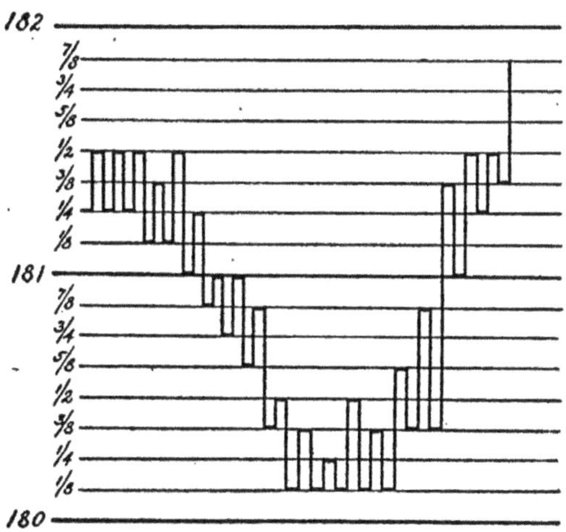

Chart showing points of resistance in a dull market

At 180⅛ a new point of resistance appears. The decline is checked. The Tape Reader must cover and go long. The steps are now upward and as the price approaches the former point of resistance he watches it narrowly for his indication to close out. This time, however, there is but slight opposition to the advance, and the price breaks through. He keeps his long stock.

A Double Stop

In making the initial trade he placed a "double" stop at 181⅝ or ¾, on the ground that if his stock overcame the resistance at 181½ it would go higher and he would have to go with it. Being short 100 shares, his double stop order would read: "Buy 200 at 181⅝ stop." Of course the price might just catch his stop and go lower. These things will happen, and anyone who cannot face them without becoming perturbed had better learn self control.

After going long around the low point, he should place another double stop at 180 or 179⅞, for if the point of resistance is broken through after he has covered and gone long, he must switch his position in an instant. Not to do so would place him in the attitude of a guesser. If he is playing on this plan he must not dilute it with other ideas.

Remember this method is only applicable to a very dull market, and, as we have said, is precarious business. We cannot recommend it. It will not as a rule pay the Tape Reader to attempt scalping fractions out of the leaders in a dull market. Commissions, tax stamps and the invisible eighth, in addition to frequent losses, form too great a handicap. There must be wide swings if profits are to exceed losses, and the thing to do is, wait for good opportunities. "The market is always with us" is an old and a true saying. We are not compelled to trade and results do not depend on *how often* we trade, but on *how much money* we make.

Trading in the Specialties

There is another way of turning a dull market to good account, and that is by trading in the stocks which are temporarily active, owing to manipulative or other causes. The Tape Reader does not care a picayune what sort of a label they put on the goods. Call a stock "Harlem Goats preferred" if you like, and make it active, preferably by means of manipulation, and the agile Tape Reader will trade in it with profit. It matters not to him whether it's a railroad or a shooting gallery; whether it declares regular or "Irish" dividends; whether the abbreviation is X Y Z or Z Y X – so long as it furnishes indications and a broad market on which to get in and out.

Take Beet Sugar on March 26, 1909, the day on which Union and Reading were so dull. It was a pipe to beat Beet Sugar. Even an embryo Tape Reader would have gone long at 30 or below, and as it never left him in doubt he could have dumped it at the top just before the close, or held it till next day, when it touched 33½.

An Example

American Beet Sugar

Shares	Price
700	29¼
200	29⅜
900	29¼
500	29⅜
700	29½
200	29⅝
900	29¾
1100	29⅞
1000	30
500	30⅛
100	30¼
100	30⅜
100	30¼
600	30⅜
1100	30½
400	30⅜
100	30¼
700	30⅜
100	30½
200	30⅜
1300	30¼
200	30⅜
300	30½
400	30⅝
100	30¾
100	30⅝
100	30½
100	30⅝
600	30½
100	30⅝
400	30½
11 A. M.	
200	30½
400	30⅝
900	30¾
100	30⅝
200	30½
200	30⅜
700	31⅞
400	32
600	32¼
600	32⅛
900	32¼
100	30½
100	30⅜
600	30½
500	30⅜
500	30½
100	30⅜
100	30¼
100	30⅜
12 M.	
200	30⅜
700	30⅛
100	30⅝
1 P. M.	
200	30¾
100	32⅝
500	30½
200	30⅝
1000	30¾
700	30⅞
600	31
600	31⅛
300	31¼
200	31⅜
100	31¼
400	31⅜
400	31½
100	31⅝
200	31⅜
200	31½
300	31⅝
200	31½
200	31⅝
200	31½
300	31⅝
2 P. M.	
100	31⅝
700	31¾
300	32⅛
400	32¼
800	32⅜
1000	32½
200	32⅝

"Get Aboard"

On March 5, 1909, Kansas City Southern spent the morning drifting between 42¾ and 43½. Shortly after the noon hour the stock burst into activity and large volume. Does any sane person suppose that a hundred or more people became convinced that Kansas City Southern was a purchase at that particular moment? What probably started the rise was the placing of manipulative orders, in which purchases predominated. Thus the sudden activity, the volume and the advancing tendency gave notice to the Tape Reader to "get aboard." The manipulator showed his hand and the Tape Reader had only to go along with the current.

Kansas City Southern

Shares	Price	Shares	Price
500	43⅜	100	43⅛
100	43½	200	43
10	43½	400	42⅞
200	43⅜	300	43¾
200	43½	100	43
100	43⅜		
100	43½	11 A. M.	
100	43¼	200	43
200	43⅛	100	42⅞
500	43	600	43
200	43⅛	25	43¼
500	43¼	100	43¼
400	43⅛	100	43⅜
100	43¼	100	43¼

Shares	Price	Shares	Price
300	43⅛	900	44⅞
500	43¼	500	45
100	43⅜	1800	44⅞
400	43¼	300	44⅝
200	43⅛	2 P. M.	
12 M.		200	44½
100	43⅜	100	44⅜
500	43½	1000	44½
100	43⅝	300	44⅝
400	43½	600	44¾
200	43⅝	100	44⅝
1200	43¾	500	44¾
400	43⅞	1200	44⅞
2300	44	200	45
1300	44⅛	100	44⅞
1400	44¼	1500	45
400	44⅜	700	45⅛
1500	[illegible]		

Shares	Price
1500	44¼
100	44⅛
400	44
1800	44⅛
200	44
800	44⅛
400	44¼
1 P. M.	
200	44¼
800	44⅜
100	44¼
300	44⅜
600	44½
100	44⅜
600	44½
800	44⅝
200	44¾
300	44⅝
200	44¾
300	44⅝
700	44¾

Shares	Price
700	45⅞
400	45¼
700	45⅛
700	45¼
300	45⅜
100	45¼
400	45⅜
900	45½
100	45⅝
700	45¾
700	45⅞
200	45¾
900	45⅞
1600	46
1400	46⅛
1000	46⅜
1300	46½
500	46⅝
200	46¾
500	46⅝
1700	46¾
300	46¾

Pyramiding

The advance was not only sustained, but emphasized at certain points. Here the Tape Reader could have pyramided, using a stop close behind his average cost and raising it so as to con-

serve profits. If he bought his first lot at 44, his second at 45, and his third at 46, he could have thrown the whole at 46⅝ and netted $406.50 for the day if he were trading in 100-share units, or $2,032.50 if trading in 500-share units.

VIII. THE USE OF CHARTS AS GUIDES AND INDICATORS

MANY interesting queries have been received by THE TICKER relating to the use of charts. The following is a representative communication:

Figure Charts

"Referring to your figure chart explained in Volume I, I have found "it a most valuable aid to detecting "accumulation or distribution in "market movements. I have been "in Wall Street a number of years, "and like many others have always "shown a skeptical attitude toward "charts and other mechanical meth- "ods of forecasting trends; but after "a thorough trial of the chart on "Union Pacific, I find that I could "have made a very considerable sum "if I had followed the indications "shown. I nee your suggestions to "operators to study earnings, etc., "and not to rely on charts, as they "are very often likely to mislead. I "regret that I cannot agree with "you. You have often stated that "the tape tells the story; since this "is true, and a chart is but a copy "of the tape, with indications of ac- ''cumulation or distribution, as the "case may be, why not follow the "chart entirely, and eliminate all unnecessary time devoted to study of "earnings, etc.?"

Let us consider those portions of the above which relate to Tape Reading, first clearly defining the difference between chart operations and tape reading.

The Chart Player

The genuine chart player usually operates in one stock at a time, using as a basis the past movements of that stock and following a more or less definite code of rules. He treats the market and his stock as a machine. He uses no judgment as to market conditions, and does not consider the movements of other stocks; but he exercises great discretion as to whether he shall "play" an indication or not.

The Tape Reader operates on what the tape shows *now.* He is not wedded to any particular issue, and, if he chooses, can work without pencil, paper or memoranda of any sort. He also has his code of rules - less clearly defined than those of the chart player. So many different situations present themselves that his rules gradually become intuitive - a sort of second nature is evolved by self-training and experience.

A friend to whom I have given some points in Tape Reading once asked if I had my rules all down so fine that I knew just which to use at certain moments. I answered him thus: When you cross a street where the traffic is heavy, do you stop to consult a set of rules showing when to run ahead of a trolley car or when not to dodge a wagon? No. You take a look both ways and at the proper moment you walk across. Your mind may be on something else or you may be reading your newspaper while crossing - your judgment tells you when to start and how fast to walk. That is the attitude of the trained Tape Reader.

The difference between the Chart Player and the Tape Reader is therefore about as wide as between day and night. We do not see how the chart follower could mix Tape Reading with his art without making a hodge-podge of it. But there are ways in which the Tape Reader may utilize charts as guides and indicators and for the purpose of reinforcing his memory.

Detecting Accumulation and Distribution

First, as our correspondent says, the Figure Chart (see TICKER, Vol. 1, No. 4) is unquestionably the best mechanical means of detecting accumulation and distribution. It is also valuable in showing the main points of resistance on the big swings.

A figure chart cannot be made from the open, high, low and last prices, such as are printed in the average newspaper. We recall but three publications from which such charts may be constructed; viz., the official N. Y. Stock Exchange list, published by F. E. Fitch, 47 Broad St, N. Y.; the N. Y. *Evening Sun,* and the *Wall Street Journal.* For general. accuracy, reliability - and economy, we prefer the Evening *Sun,* which costs, postpaid, only 20 cents a month, or $2 a year.

Figure Chart of Amalgamated Copper During the 1903 Panic

We produce a Figure Chart of Amalgamated Copper showing movements during the 1903 panic and up to the following March (1904). It makes an interesting study. The stock sold early in the year at 75⅝ and the low point reached during the above period was 33⅝ The movements prior to those recorded here show a series of downward steps; but. when 36 is reached, the formation changes, and the supporting points are raised. A seven-point rally, a reaction to almost the low figure, and another sixteen- point rally follow.

On this rally the lines 48-49 gradually form the axis and long rows of these figures seem to indicate that plenty of stock is for sale at this level. In case we are not sure as to whether this is further accumulation or distribution we wait until the price shows signs of breaking out of this narrow range. After the second run up to 51 ' the gradually lowering tops warn us that pressure is resumed. We therefore look for lower prices.

Interpreting the Chart

The downward steps continue till 35 is touched, where a 36-7 line begins to form. There is a dip to 33⅝, which gives us the full figure 34, after which the bottoms are higher and lines commence forming at 38-9. Here are all the earmarks of manipulative depression and accumulation – the stock is not allowed to rally over 39 until liquidation is complete. Then the gradually raised bottoms notify us in advance that the stock is about to push through to higher levels.

Now if the Figure Chart were an infallible guide no one would have to learn anything more than its correct interpretation in order to make big money. Our correspondent says, "after a thorough trial of the chart on U. P. I find that I could have made a very considerable sum if I had followed the indications shown." But he would not have followed the indications shown. He is fooling himself. It is easy to look over the chart afterwards and see where he could have made correct plays, but I venture to say he never tested the plan under proper conditions.

Make a Test

Let anyone who thinks he can make money following a Figure Chart or any other kind of a chart have a friend prepare it, keeping secret the name of the stock and the period covered. Then put down on paper a positive set of rules which are to be strictly adhered to, so that there can be no guesswork. Each situation will then call for a certain play and no deviation is to be allowed. Cover up with a sheet of paper all but the beginning of the chart, gradually sliding the paper to the right as you progress. Record each order and execution just as if actually trading. Put Rollo Tape down as coppering every trade and when done send him a check for what you have lost.

I have yet to. meet the man who has made money trading on a Figure Chart over an extended period.

Any kind of a chart will show some profits at times, but the test is: How much money will it make during several months' operations?

The Figure Chart can be used in other ways. Some people construct figure charts showing each fractional change instead of the full points. The idea may also be used in connection with the Dow, Jones & Co. average prices. But for the practical Tape Reader the full figure chart first described is about the only one we can recommend.

Its value to the Tape Reader lies chiefly in its indications of accumulation and distribution. These frequently (not always) warn the operator in advance of an important move and put him on the watch for the moment when either process is completed and the marking up or down begins.

The chart gives the direction of coming moves; the tape says "when."

Many Exceptions

Some people claim to be able to predict how far such a movement will go by counting the number of full figures which form an unbroken line. In a case where a stock shows a long horizontal line of 19s and 20s at the bottom of a decline, and a count of the 20s shows that there are twelve of them, this is taken as an indication that there will be a rise of twelve points from 20. Figure charts seem to bear this out in some instances, but like the majority of chart indications, there are very many exceptions to the rule. There appears some little foundation for the supposition, however, as it is logical to suppose that the more important the contemplated move, the more stock will the insiders wish to buy and the longer time will be required in which to accumulate it.

The ordinary single line chart which is so widely used, is valuable chiefly as a compact history of a stock's movements. If the stock which is charted were the only one in the market, its gyrations would be less erratic and its chart, therefore, a more reliable indicator of its trend and destination. But we must keep before us the incontrovertible fact that the movements of every stock are to a greater or lesser extent affected by those of every other stock. This in a large measure accounts for the instability of stock movements as recorded in single line charts.

Reciprocal Influences

Then, too, as shown in foregoing studies in this series, one stock may be the lever with which the whole market is being held up, or the club with which the general list is being pounded. A chart of the pivotal stock might give a strong buying indication, whereupon the blind chart devotee would go long to his ultimate regret; for when the concealed distribution was completed his stock would probably break quickly and badly.

This shows clearly the advantage of Tape Reading over chart playing. The Tape Reader sees everything that is going on; the chart player's vision is limited to one issue. Both aim to get in right and go with the trend, but the eye that comprehends the market as a whole is the one which can read this trend most accurately.

A Composite Chart

If one wishes a mechanical trend indicator as a supplement and a guide to his Tape Reading, he had best keep a chart composed of the average daily high and low of eight or ten leading stocks. For convenience in figuring this average it is well to take ten stocks, say Union, Reading, St. Paul, Pennsylvania, N. Y. Central and Erie among the railroads, and Amalgamated, Smelters, Steel and Car Foundry among the industrials. First find the average high and average low for the day and make a chart showing which was touched first. This will be found a more reliable guide than the Dow, Jones averages, which only consider the closing bid of each day, and which, as strongly illustrated in the May, 1901, panic, frequently do not fairly represent the day's actual fluctuations.

Such a composite chart is of no value to the Tape Reader who scalps and closes out everything daily. But it should benefit those who read the tape for the purpose of catching the important five or ten point moves. Such a trader will make no commitments not in accordance with the trend, as shown by this chart. His reason is that even a well planned bull campaign in a stock will not usually be pushed to completion in the face of a down trend in the general market. Therefore he waits until the trend conforms to his indication.

It seems hardly necessary to say that an up trend in any chart is indicated by consecutive higher tops and bottoms, like stairs going up, and the reverse by repeated steps toward a lower level. A series of tops or bottoms at the same level shows resistance. A protracted zig-zag within a short radius accompanied by very small volume means lifelessness, but with normal or abnormally large volume, accumulation or distribution is more or less evidenced.

There is a style of chart which was originated by "The Analyst," it being especially adapted to the study of volumes. The following rough sketch will give an idea of it:

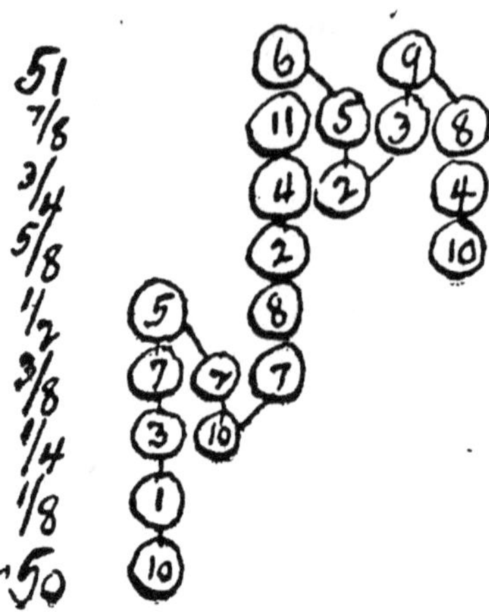

Volume Chart

When made to cover a day's movements in a stock, this chart is particularly valuable in showing the quantity of stock absorbed at various levels. Comparisons are readily made by adding the quantities horizontally. Many other suggestions will be derived from the study of this chart.

Dividends

An important point in connection with the making of charts is the treatment of a stock which sells ex-dividend. Many people consider a dividend as equal to a corresponding decline in market price; in fact, the most prominent publisher of charts follows this method. We do not agree. In our opinion when a stock sells ex-dividend the scale should be changed so that the stock will show the same relative position as before the dividend. For instance, if a stock is 138 before a dividend amounting to 2 per cent and sells at 136 ex-dividend, the 138 line becomes the 136 line, etc.

There is another form of chart which is sometimes valuable in detecting the beginning and end of a manipulative campaign. It is based principally on volumes and affords a ready indicator of any unusual activity in a stock. The scale is set at the side to represent the volume and the vertical lines are drawn to show the number of shares for the day. A plus or minus sign at the top of each vertical line may be used to indicate a net advance or decline for the day. Some people add to this an oblique line to show the range for the day.

The proficient Tape Reader will doubtless prefer to discard all mechanical helps, because they interfere with his sensing the trend. Besides, if he keeps the charts himself the very act of running them distracts his attention from the tape on which his eye should be constantly riveted. This can of course be overcome by employing an assistant; but taking everything into consideration – the division of attention, the contradictions and the confusing situations which will frequently result – we advise students to stand free of mechanical helps so far as it is possible.

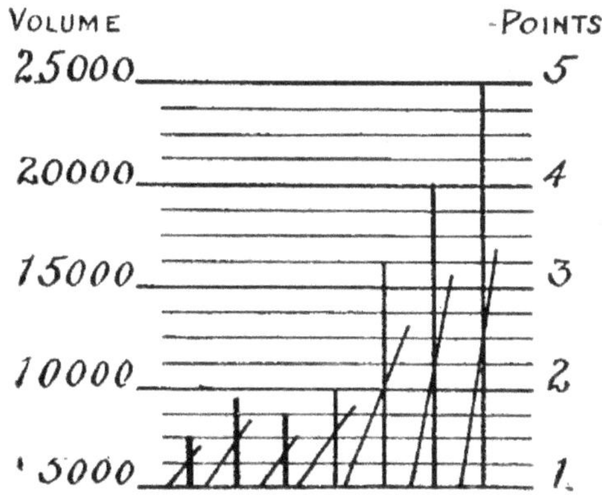

Chart Showing Daily Volume and Width of Swing

Stick to the Tape

Our correspondent in saying "a chart is but a copy of the tape" doubtless refers to the chart of one stock. The full tape cannot possibly be charted. The tape does tell the story, but charting one or two stocks is like recording the actions of one individual as exemplifying the actions of a very large family.

IX.
DAILY TRADES VS. LONG PULL OPERATIONS

JUST now I took a small triangular piece of blotting paper three-eighths of an inch at its widest, and stuck it on the end of a pin. I then threw a blot of ink on a paper and put the blotter into contact. The ink fairly jumped up into the blotter, leaving the paper comparatively dry.

Absorption

This is exactly how the market acts on the tape when its absorptive powers are greater than the supply - large quantities are taken at the offered prices and at the higher levels. Prices leap forward. The demand seems insatiable.

After two or three blots had thus been absorbed, the botter would take no more. It was thoroughly saturated. Its demands were satisfied. Just in this way the market comes to a standstill at the top of a rise and hangs there. Supply and demand are equalized at the new price level.

Then I filled my pen with ink, and let the fluid run off the point and onto the blotter. (This illustrated the distribution of stocks in the market) Be yond a certain point the blotter would take no more. A drop formed and fell to the paper. (Supply exceeded demand.) The more I put on the blotter the faster fell the drops. (Liquidation - market seeking a lower level.)

This is a simple way of fixing in our minds the principal opposing - forces that are constantly operating in the market - absorption and distribution, demand and supply, support and pressure. The more adept a Tape Reader becomes in weighing and measuring these elements, the more successful he will be.

Watchfulness

But he must remember that even his most accurate readings will often be nullified by events which are transpiring every moment of the day. His stock may start upward with a rush – apparently there is power enough to carry it several points; but after advancing a couple of points it may run up against a larger quantity of stock than can be obsorbed, or some unforeseen incident may change the whole complexion of the market. The Tape Reader must be quick to detect such changes, switch his position and go with this newly formed trend.

To show how an operator may be caught twice on the wrong side in one day and still come out ahead, let us look at the tape of December 21, 1908.

Union Pacific opened below the previous night's close: 500 . 179 . 6000 . 178¾ and for the first few moments looked, as though there was some inside support. Supposing, the. Tape Reader had

BOUGHT 100 UNION PACIFIC AT 178⅞, he would have soon noticed fresh selling orders in sufficient volume to produce weakness. Upon this he would have immediately

A Mistake

SOLD 200 UNION PACIFIC AT 178¼, putting him short one hundred at the latter price. The weakness increased and after a drive to 176%, two or three warnings were given that the pressure was temporarily off. A comparatively strong undertone developed in Southern Pacific as well as other stocks and short covering began in Union Pacific, which came 600 . 176⅝ . 1000 . 54, then 177¼. Assuming that the operator considered this the turn, he would have

BOUGHT 200 UNION PACIFIC AT 176%, which was the next quotation. This would have put him long. Thereafter the market showed more resiliency, but only small lots appeared on the tape.

A little later the market quiets down. The rally does not hold well. He expects the stock to react again to the low point. This it does, but it fails to halt there; it goes driving through to 176, accompanied by • considerable weakness in the other active stocks. This is his indication that fresh liquidation has started. So he

SELLS 200 UNION PACIFIC AT 176. That is he dumps over his long and goes short at 176.

The weakness continues and there is no sign of a rally until after the stock has struck 174%. This being* a break of 6¼ points since yesterday, the Tape Reader is now wide awake for signs of a turn, realizing that every additional fraction brings him nearer to that point, wherever it may be.

After touching 174½ the trend of the market changes completely. Larger lots are in demand at the offered prices. There is a final drive but very little stock comes out on it. During this drive he

Catching the Turn

BUYS 100 UNION PACIFIC AT 174⅞. and as signs of a rally multiply he

BUYS 100 UNION PACIFIC AT 175¼. From that moment it is easy sailing. There is ample opportunity for him to unload his last purchase just before the close when he

SELLS 100 UNION PACIFIC AT 176⅝.

Bought.	Sold.	Loss.	Profit.
178⅞	178¼	$62.50	......
176⅞	178¼	......	$137.50
176⅞	176	87.50	......
174⅞	176	......	112.50
175¼	176⅝	......	137.50
Commissions and taxes......		135.00	......
		$285.00	$387.50
			285.00
Net profit for the day			$102.50

This is doing very well considering he was caught twice on the wrong side and in his wigglings paid $135 in commissions and taxes.

Waiting for the Trend

Success in trading being chiefly a question of reducing and eliminating losses, commissions, interest and revenue stamps, let us see whether he might have used better judgment. His first trade seems to have been made on what appeared to be inside buying. No trend had developed. He saw round lots being taken at 178¾ and over and reasoned that a rally should naturally follow pronounced support. His mistake was in not waiting for a clearly defined trend. If the buying was strong enough to absorb all offerings and turn the market, he would have done better to have waited till this was certain. When a stock holds steady within a half point radius it does not signify a reversal of trend, but rather a halting place from which a new move in either direction may begin.

Had he followed the first sharp move, his original trade would have been on the short - not the long side. This would have saved him his first loss with its attendant expenses, aggregating $89.50, and would have nearly doubled the day's profits.

His second loss was made on a trade which involved one of the finest points in the art of Tape Reading, viz., that of distinguishing a rally from a change in trend. A good way to do this successfully is to figure where a stock is due to come after it makes an upturn, allowing that a normal rally is from one-half to two-thirds of the decline." That is, when a stock declines two and a half points we can look for at least a point and a quarter rally unless the pressure is still on. In case the decline is not over, the rally will fall short.

Distinguishing a Mere Rally

What did Union do after it touched 176½ ? It sold at 176⅝ . ¾ . 177¼. Having declined from 179⅛ to 176½, 2⅝ points, it was due to rally at least 1% points, or to 177¾. Its failing to make this figure indicated that the decline was not over and that his short position should be maintained.

Furthermore, that last jump of half a point between sales showed an unhealthy condition of the market. For a few moments there was evidently a cessation of selling, then somebody reached for a hundred shares offered at 177¼. As the next sale was 176⅞. the hollowness of the rise became apparent.

While this rally lasted, the lots were small. This of itself was reason for not covering. Had a. genuine demand sprung from either longs or shorts a steady rise, on increasing volumes, would have taken place. The absence of such indications seems to us now a reason for hot covering and going long at 176⅞.

Studying Losses

It is very difficult for anyone to say what he would actually have done under the circumstances, but had both these trades been avoided for the reasons mentioned, the profit for the day would have been $421, as the 100 sold at 178¼ would have been covered at 174⅞, and the long at 175¼ sold out at 176⅝. So we can see the advantage of studying our losses and mistakes, with a view to benefiting in future transactions.

As previously explained, the number of dollars profit is subordinate to whether the trader can- make profits at all and whether the points made exceed the points lost. With success from this standpoint it is only a question of increased capital enabling one to enlarge his trading unit.

A good way to watch the progress of an account is to keep a book showing dates, quantities, prices, profits and losses, also commission, tax and interest charges. Beside each trade should be entered the number of points net profit or loss, together with a running total showing just how many points the account is ahead or behind. A chart of these latter figures will prevent anyone fooling himself as to his progress. People are too apt to remember their profits and forget their losses.

Small Losses

The losses taken by an expert Tape Reader are so small that he can trade in much larger units than one who is away from the tape or who is trading with an arbitrary stop. The Tape Reader will seldom take over half a point to a point loss for the reason that he will generally buy or sell at, or close to, the pivotal point or the line of resistance. Therefore, should the trend of his stock suddenly reverse, he is with it in a moment. The losses in the above mentioned Union Pacific transactions (⅝ and ⅞ respectively) are perhaps a fair average, but frequently he will be able to trade with a risk of only ¼, ⅜ or ½.

The fact that this possible loss is confined to a fraction should not lead him to trade too frequently. It is better to look on part of the time; to rest the mind and allow the judgment to clarify. Dull days will often constrain one for a time and are therefore beneficial.

The big money in Tape Reading is made during very active markets. Big swings and large volumes produce unmistakable indications and a harvest for the experienced operator. He welcomes twenty, thirty and fifty-point moves in stocks like Reading, Union or Consolidated Gas – powerful plays by financial giants.

And this fact reminds us of one of the things we have heretofore intended to reason out: Is it better to close trades each day, or hold through reactions, and if necessary, for several days or weeks in order to secure a large profit?

Difference in Individuals

The answer to this question depends somewhat upon the temperament of the Tape Reader. If his make-up is such that he can closely follow the small swings with profit, gradually becoming more expert and steadily increasing his commitments, he will shortly "arrive" by that route. If his disposition is such that he cannot trade in and out actively, but is content to wait for big opportunities and patient enough to hold on for large profits, he will also "get there." It is impossible to say which style of trading would produce the best average results, because it depends altogether upon individual qualifications.

Looking at the question broadly, we should say that the Tape Reader who understood the lines thus far suggested in this series, might find it both difficult and less profitable to operate solely for the long swings. In the first place, he would be obliged to let twenty or thirty opportunities pass by to every one that he would accept. The small swings of one to three points greatly outnumber the five and ten- point movements, and there would be a considerable percentage of losing trades no matter how he operated.

Trading for the Long Swings

It would seem also that close contact with the ticket would not give the correct perspective for long pull operations. Many of the indications, such as the extent of reactions, lines of resistance, etc., will be found equally operative in the broader swings, just as an enlargement of a photograph retains the lines of its original. Tape Reading seems essentially a profession for the man who is mentally active and flexible, capable of making quick and accurate decisions and keenly sensitive to the most minute indications. On the other hand, trading for the larger swings requires one to ignore the -minor prognostics, and to put some stress upon the influential news of the day, and its effect upon sentiment; he must stand ready. to take larger losses and in many ways handle himself in a manner altogether different from that of the small swing trader.

The more closely we look at the proposition, the more the two methods of operating seem to disunite, the broad swing plan appearing best adapted to those who are not in continuous touch with the ticker and who therefore have the advantage of distance and perspective.

In, a subsequent series we hope to take up this subject in detail, in an effort to show how the business and the professional man who cannot attend his broker's office, may profitably apply intelligent foresight to the stock market under the shade of his evening lamp.

Auxiliary Trades

There is no reason why the Tape Reader should not make long swing trading an auxiliary profit producer if he can keep such trades from influencing his daily operations.

For example, in the recent shakedown on Reading from 144⅜ to 118, on his first buying indication he could have taken on an extra lot for the long swing, knowing that if the turn had really been made, a rally to over 130 was due. A stop order would have limited his risk and conserved his profits as they rolled up and there is no telling how much of the subsequent forty point rise he might have secured.

Another case was when Steel broke from 58¾ last November (1908) to 41¼ in February. The market at the time was hinging on Steel and it was likely that the Tape Reader would be operating in it. His first long trade under this plan would be for at least a hundred shares more than his usual amount, with a stop on the long pull lot at say 40¾. He would naturally expect a rally of at least 8¾ points (to 50), but would, in a sense, forget this hundred shares, so long as the market showed no signs of another important decline. When it reached 60 he might still be holding it.

The above are merely a couple of opportunities from recent stock market history. Dozens of such openings show themselves every year and should form no small part of the Tape Reader's income. But he must separate such trades from his regular daily trading; to allow them to conflict would destroy the effectiveness of both. If he finds the long pull trade interfering with the accuracy of his judgment, he should close it out at once. He must play on one side of the fence if he cannot operate on both.

A Dual Capacity

One can readily foresee how a trader with one hundred shares of Steel at 43 for the long pull, and two hundred for the day, would be tempted to close out all three hundred on indications of a decline. This is where he can test his ability to act in a dual capacity. He must ask himself: Have I good reason for thinking Steel will sell down five points before up five ? Is this a small reaction or a big shakedown? Are we still in a bull swing? Has the stock had its normal rally from the last decline? These and many other questions will enable him to decide whether he should hold this hundred shares or clean house.

It takes an exceptionaly strong will and clear head to act in this way without interfering with one's regular trading. Anyone can sell two hundred and hold one hundred; but will his judgment be biased because he is simultaneously long and short - bullish and bearish ? There's the rub!

Advantage of a Clean Slate

The real Tape Reader is apt to pre fer a clean slate at 3 P. M. every day, so that he can sit down to his ticker at the next morning's opening and say, "I have no commitments and no opinion. I will follow the first strong indication." He would rather average $100 a day for ten days than make $1,000 on one trade in the same length of time. The risk is generally limited to a fraction and having arrived at a point where he is showing even small average daily profits, his required capital per 100 shares need not be over $1,500 to $2,000.

Suppose for sixty days on 100- share operations his average profits over losses were only a quarter of a point - $25 a day. At the end of that time his capital would have been increased by $1,500, enabling him to trade in 200 share lots. Another thirty days with similar results and he could trade in 300-share lots, and so on. I do not mention these figures for any other purpose than to again emphasize that the objective point in Tape Reading is not large individual profits, but a continuous chipping in of small average net profits per day.

An Incident

About two months ago, I am told, a man from the West came into the office of THE TICKER, and said that he had been impressed by this series on Tape Reading, and had come to New York for the sole purpose of trying his hand at it. He had $1,000 which he was willing to lose in demonstrating whether he was fitted for the work.

He was advised not to trade in over ten-share lots, and was especially warned against operating at all until after he had actually studied the tape for two or three months.

Recently, I am informed, he called again and related some of his experiences. It seems that he could not abstain from trading, but started within two or three days after he decided on a brokerage house. He stated that during the two months he had made forty-two trades of ten shares each and had never had on hand over twenty full shares at any one time. He admitted that he had frequently mixed guesswork and tips with his Tape Reading, but as a rule he had followed the tape.

His losses were seldom over a point and his greatest loss was one and a half points. His maximum profit was three points. He had at times traded in other stocks beside the leaders. In spite of his inexperience, and his attempt to mix tips and guesses with shrewd judgment, he was actually ahead of the game, after paying out about $125 in commissions, etc.

This was especially surprising in view of the trader's market through which he had passed. While the amount of his net profit was small, the fact that he had shown any profit under the circumstances was reason enough for congratulation.

Another handicap which he did not perhaps realize was his environment. He had been trading in an office where he could hear and see what everyone else was doing, and where news, gossip and opinions were freely and openly expressed by many people.. All these things tended to influence him, and to switch him from his Tape Reading.

Cutting Losses

I have no doubt that having mastered the art of cutting losses and keeping commitments down, he will soon overcome his other deficiencies. Given a broad, active market, he should show increasing average daily profits.

He is creeping now. By-and-by he will know how to walk.

Speculation is a business. It must be learned.

X. VARIOUS EXAMPLES AND SUGGESTIONS

RECENT trading observations and experiments have convinced me that it is impracticable and almost impossible to gauge the extent of a movement by its initial fluctuations.

Gauging the Swing

Many important swings begin in the most modest way. The top of an important decline may present nothing more than a light volume and a drifting tendency toward lower prices, subsequently developing into a heavy, slumpy market, and ending in a violent downward plunge.

In a previous number I suggested that the Tape Reader select only those moves which seem to offer opportunities for wide swings. My opinion now is that the operator should aim to catch every important swing in the leading active stock. To do this he must act promptly when a stock goes into a new field or otherwise gives an indication, and he must be ready to follow wherever it leads. If it has been moving within a three-point radius and suddenly takes on new life and activity, bursting through its former bounds, he must go with it.

I do not mean that he should try to catch every wriggle. If the stock rises three points and then reverses one or one and a half points on light volume, he must look upon it as a perfectly natural reaction and not a change of trend. The expert operator will not ordinarily let all of three points get away from him. He will keep pushing his stop up behind until the first good reaction puts him out at close to the high figure. This leaves him in a position to repurchase on the reaction, provided no better opportunity presents itself. Having purchased at such a time, he will sell out again as the price once more approaches the high figure, unless indications point to its forging through to a new high level.

Stages of Market Movements

Every movement of the market and of each stock passes through stages corresponding to those in the life of an individual, aptly described by my old college chum, Bill Shakespeare, as "The Seven Ages." The Tape Reader aims to get in during Infancy and out at Old Age.

Usually a movement gives signs when it begins to totter. A recent example was given in the rise in Union Pacific about June 21st to 23d (1909), when the stock rose from 187⅞ to accompanied by an abnormal advance in the preferred. Each morning the London price for both issues came higher and there was persistent buying all day in the New York market. After touching 194⅝ the movement completely fizzled out. Buying pressure ceased. The preferred reacted sharply, and the common came back to 193⅞ Thereafter its rallies were feeble, the pressure was all on the down side, and today, June 26th, it is still heavy at 191⅞.

A new bull movement may have its birth during great weakness or pressure. Just prior to the above time, Reading was pounded down to 147⅝, then to 147¼, and the resistance which it offered at this level gave notice that a new swing was about to be inaugurated. These were signs that the Tape Reader had better get bullish. Purchases could have been made with only a fractional risk, and subsequent profits were chiefly on the bull side. Two or three days later the price touched 155½, then it went above 158.

Importance of Volumes

The more we study volumes, the better we appreciate their value in Tape Reading. It frequently occurs that a stock will work within a three- point range for days at a time without giving one a chance for a respectablesized scalp. Without going out of these boundaries, it suddenly begins coming out on the tape in thousands instead of hundreds. This is evidence that a new movement has started, but not necessarily in the direction which is first indicated. The Tape Reader must immediately go with the trend, but until it is clearly defined and the stock breaks through its former limits with large and increasing volumes, he must exercise great caution. The reason is this: If the stock has been suddenly advanced, it may be for the purpose of facilitating sales by a large operator. The Tape is the most suggestive thing in the world. A sharp rise of this kind induces a number of people to buy;. their buying attracts others and as the tide swells it carries all before it until everybody throws caution aside and jumps in. Thus we see a cross section of a pyramid formed by outsiders working *en masse.* A legitimate movement of this kind will frequently run several points. The large operator who wishes to unload a block of stock or put out a big line of shorts, creates an illegitimate move, inducing others to buy and making a market for what he wishes to dispose of. The best way to distinguish the genuine from the fictitious move is to watch out for abnormally large volumes within a small radius. This usually evidences washed sales and other manipulations. The large volume is simply a means of attracting buyers and disguising the hand of the operator.

Cross Section of a Movement

A play of this kind took place the last time Reading struck 159¾ (June, 1909). I counted some 80,000 shares within about half a point of 159 – unmistakable notice of a coming decline. This was a case where the stock was put up before being put down, and the Tape Reader who interpreted the move correctly and played for a good down swing would have made considerable money.

The Public

We frequently hear people complaining that "the public is not in this market," as though that were a reason why stocks should not go up or the market should be avoided. The speaker is usually one of those who constitute "the public," but he regards the expression as signifying "every outsider except myself." In the judgment of many the market is better off without the public. To be sure, brokers do not enjoy so large a business, the fluctuations are not so riotous, but the market moves in an orderly way and responds more accurately to prevailing conditions.

A market in which the public predominates represents a sort of speculative "jag" indulged in by those whose stock market knowledge should be rated at 1/8. Everyone recognizes the fact that when the smoke clears away, the Street is full of victims who didn't know how and couldn't wait to learn. Their plungings produce violent fluctuations, however, and in this respect are of advantage to the Tape Reader who would much rather see ten-point than three-point swings.

Execution of Orders

To offset this, there are some disadvantages. First, in a market where there is "rioting of accumulated margins," the tape is so far behind that it is seldom one can secure an execution at anywhere near his price. This is especially true when activity breaks out in a stock which has been comparatively dull. So many people with money, watching the tape, are attracted by these apparent opportunities, that the scramble to get in results in every one paying more than he figured; thus the Tape Reader finds it impossible to know where he is at until he gets his report. His tape prices are five minutes stale and his broker is so busy it takes four or five minutes for an execution instead of one or two minutes.

In the next place, stop orders are often filled at from small fractions to points away from his stop price - there is no telling what figure he will get, while in ordinary markets he can place his stops within 1/4 of a resistance point and frequently have the price come within 1/8 of his stop without catching it.

So it is a question whether, all things considered, the presence of the public is a help or a detriment to successful Tape Reading.

Stop Orders

Speaking of stop orders: The ways in which one may manipulate his stops for protection and advantage, become more numerous as experience is acquired. ' Remembering that the Tape Reader is operating for a fractional average profit per trade, or per day, he cannot afford to let a point profit run into a loss, or fail to "plug" a larger profit at a point where at least a portion of it will be preserved. '

One of my recent day's trading will illustrate this idea. I had just closed out a couple of trades, in which there had been losses totaling slightly over a point. Both were on the long side. The market began to show signs of a break, and singling out Reading as the most vulnerable, I got short of it at 150¾ In a few moments it sold below 150. My stop was moved down so there couldn't be a loss, and soon a slight rally and another break gave me a new stop which insured a profit, come what might. A third drive started, and I pushed the stop down to within ¼ of the tape price at the time, as it was late in the day and I considered this the final plunge. By the time my order reached the floor the price was well away from this latest stop and when the selling became most violent I told my broker to cover "at the market." The price paid was within ¼ of the bottom for the day, and netted 2⅝ after commissions were paid.

Elimination of Losses

I strongly advocate this method of profit insuring. The scientific elimination of loss is one of the most, important factors in the art, and the operator who fails to properly protect his paper profits will find that many a point which he thought he had cinched has slipped away from him.

It is also a question whether, in such a case, the trade had better not be stopped out than closed out. When you push a stop close behind a rise or a decline, you leave the way open for a further profit; but when you close the trade of your own volition, you shut off all such chances. If it is your habit to close out everything before three o'clock daily, the stop may be placed closer than ordinarily during the last fifteen minutes of the session, and when a sharp move in the desired direction occurs, the closing out may be done by a stop only a fraction away from the extreme price. This whole plan of using stops is a sort of squeezing out the last drop of profit from each trade and never losing any part that can possibly be retained.

Suppose the operator sells a stock short at 53 and it breaks to 51. He is foolish not to bring his stop down to 51¼ unless the market is ripe for a heavy decline. With his stop at this point he has two chances out of three that the result will be satisfactory: (1) The price may go lower and yield a further profit; (2) The normal rally to 52 will catch his stop and enable him to put the stock out again at that price. The third contingency is that it will rally to about 51¼, catch his stop and then go lower. He can scarcely mourn over the loss of a further profit in such a case.

Scalping on Both Sides

If the stock refuses to rally the full point to which it is entitled, that is, if it comes up to 51½ or ⅝ and still acts heavy, it may be expected to break lower, and there usually is ample time to get short again at a price that will at least cover commissions.

There is nothing more confusing than to attempt scalping on both sides of the market at once. You may go long of a stock which is being put up or is going up for some special reason, and short of another stock which is persistently weak. Both trades may pan out successfully, but meantime the judgment will be interfered with and some foolish mistake will be made in four cases out of five. As Dickson G. Watts said, "Act so as to keep the mind clear, the judgment trustworthy." The mind is not clear when the trader is working actively on two opposing sides of the market. A bearish indication is favorable to one trade, and unfavorable to the other. He finds himself interpreting every development as being to his advantage and forgetting the important fact that he is also on the opposite side.

It is much better if you are short of one stock and see another that looks like a purchase, to wait until you have covered your short trade (on a dip if possible), and then take the long side of the other issue. The best time for both covering and going long is on a recession which in such a case serves a double purpose. The mind should be made up in advance as to which deal offers the best chance for profit, so that when the moment for action arrives there will be nothing to do but act.

Getting in

This is one great advantage the Tape Reader has over other operators who do not employ market science. By a process of elimination he decides which side of the market and which stock affords the best opportunity. He either gets in at the inception of a movement or waits for the first reaction after the move has started. He knows just about where his stock will come on the reaction and judges by the way it then acts whether his first impression is confirmed or nullified. After he gets in it must come up to expectations or he should abandon the trade. If it is a bull move, the volume must increase and the rest of the market offer some support or at least not oppose it. The reactions must show a smaller volume than the advances, indicating light pressure, and each upward swing must be of longer duration and reach a new high level, or it will mean that the rise has spent its force either temporarily or finally.

Advantages of Tape Reading

Tape Reading is the only known method of trading which gets you in at the beginning, keeps you posted throughout the move, and gets you out when it has culminated.

If anything more approaching perfection in this regard exists will someone kindly come to the front with it?

Has anyone ever heard of a man, a method, system, or anything else that that will do this for you in Wall Street?

It has made fortunes for the comparatively few who have followed it.

It is an art in which one can become highly expert and more and more successful as practice and experience sandpapers his work and shows him what to avoid.

I should like to hear from my readers who have followed this series, whether they have been operating under its guidance or not. I should like to know how many have started to perfect themselves in Tape Reading, and how many have been aided indirectly; what portions and which ideas have benefited them most; what points are not clear or still -uncovered. Please write me fully and I will try to answer in the two subsequent numbers, which will close the series. Address Rollo Tape, care of THE TICKER.

XI. OBSTACLES TO BE OVERCOME – POSSIBLE PROFITS

MENTAL poise is an indispensable factor in Tape Reading. The mind should be absolutely free to concentrate upon the work; there should be no feeling that certain things are to be accomplished within a given time; no fear, anxiety or ambition.

When a Tape Reader has his emotions well in hand, he will play as though the game were dominoes. When anything interferes with this attitude it should be eliminated. If, for example, there be an unusual series of losses, the trader had better suspend operations until he discovers the cause.

Following are some of the obstacles which are likely to be encountered:

Trading Too Often

1. One may be trading too often. Many opportunities for profit develop from each day's movements; only the very choicest should be acted upon. There should be no haste. The market will be there to-morrow in case to-day's opportunities do not meet requirements.

2. Anxiety to make a record, to avoid losses, to secure a certain profit for the day or period will greatly warp the judgment, and lead to a low percentage of profits. Tape Reading is a good deal like laying eggs. If the hen is not left to pick up the necessary foods and retire in peace to her nest, she will not produce properly. If she is worried by dogs and small boys, or tries to lay seven eggs out of material for six, the net proceeds may look like an omelet.

The Tape Reader's profits should develop naturally. He should buy or sell because it is the thing to do – not because he wants to make a profit or fears to make a loss.

3. The market may be unsuited to Tape Reading operations. When prices drift up and down without trend, like a ship without a rudder, and few positive indications develop, the percentage of los-

ing trades is apt to be high. When this condition continues it is well to hold off until the character of the market changes.

Poor Service

4. One's broker may be giving poor service. In a game as fine as this, every fraction counts. Executions of market orders should average not over two minutes. Stop orders should be reported in less time as such orders are on the floor and at the proper post when they become operative. By close attention to details in the handling of my orders, I have been able to reduce the average time of my executions to less than one minute. The quickest report obtained thus far required but twenty-five seconds. To the best of my knowledge this is a record for New York Stock Exchange executions of orders given from an office.

A considerable portion of my orders ate executed in from thirty to forty seconds, varying according to whether my broker is near the 'phone or in a distant crowd when the orders reach the floor and how far the definitive "crowd" is from his 'phone.

I have arranged a special order slip which distinguishes my orders. It reads:

Special Order Slip

BUY AT THE OFFERED PRICE AND REPORT INSTANTLY

The selling slips read, *"Sell at the bid price and report instantly."* Such orders leave nothing to the discretion of the broker. He cannot "try to do better" than the momentary bid or offered price. Like Paddy at the wake, his business is to "hit the first man who opens his mouth."

The Broker's Discretion

Ordinarily it is expected and is really an advantage to the general run of speculators to have the broker use some discretion; that is, try to do better, providing there is no chance of losing his market. But I do not wish my broker to act thus for me. My indications usually show me the exact moment when a stock should be bought or sold and a few moments' delay often means a good many dollars lost.

With the execution of orders reduced to a matter of seconds, I can also hold stop orders in my own hands and when the stop price is reached, 'phone the order to buy or sell at the market. Results are very satisfactory as my own broker handles the orders and not the specialist or some other floor broker.

To return to the question of mental equilibrium, the Tape Reader should be careful to trade only in such amounts as will not interfere with his judgment. If he finds that a series of losses upsets him it is an easy matter to reduce the number of shares one-half or a quarter of the regular amount, or even to ten shares so that the dollars involved are no longer a factor. This gives him a chance for a little self-examination.

If a person is in poor physical condition or his mental alertness below par for any reason, he may be unable to stand the excitement attending the work. Loss of sleep, for example, may render one unfit to carry all the quotations in his head, or to plan and execute his moves quickly and accurately. When anything of this kind occurs which prevents the free play of all the faculties it is best to bring the day's work to a close.

Fractional Profits

Some of my readers think it futile to aim for a fractional average profit per trade when there are many full points per day to be made by holding on through days and weeks and getting full benefit of the big moves. Admitting that it is possible to make many more points at times there is a risk of losses corresponding to the profits and the question is not how much we can *make,* but how much we can make *net.*

Tape Reading reduces profit-making to a manufacturing basis.

To show how the nimble eighths pile up when their cumulative power is fully employed, I have prepared a table representing the results of 250 trading days, starting with a capital of $1,000. It is assumed that the Tape Reader has reached that stage of expertness where he can average one trade a day and a profit of $12.50 per trade, and that as fast as $1,000 is accumulated he adds 100 shares to his trading unit.

I can hear the expressions of. those who look over these figures: "Oh! That looks all very well on paper, but wait till it comes to doing it in the market."

The Nimble Eighth

These results depend solely upon the Tape Reader's ability to make ⅛ more than he loses per day. There is no limit to the number of shares he can trade in, provided he has the margin. If he is at all proficient his margin will not be depleted more than a few points before he makes up his losses and more. He is not pyramiding in the ordinary sense of the word; he is simply doing an increasing volume of shares as his capital expands. All progressive business men increase commitments as fast as warranted by their capital and opportunities.

What a profit of 1-8 per day would amount to in 250 days if profits were used as additional margin.

100	shares	$12.50	a day	$1,000.00	in	80	days
200	"	25.00	"	1,000.00	"	40	"
300	"	37.50	"	1,012.50	"	27	"
400	"	50.00	"	1,000.00	"	20	"
500	"	62.50	"	1,000.00	"	16	"
600	"	75.00	"	1,050.00	"	14	"
700	"	87.50	"	1,050.00	"	12	"
800	"	100.00	"	1,000.00	"	10	"
900	"	112.50	"	1,012.50	"	9	"
1000	"	125.00	"	1,000.00	"	8	"
1100	"	137.50	"	962.50	"	7	"
1200	"	150.00	"	1,050.00	"	7	"
				$12,137.50	"	250	"
Less tax				1,942.00			
Net profit				$10,195.50			

Overcoming the "Kitty"

Assuming that there are about three hundred Stock Exchange sessions in the year, the two hundred and fifty days figured represent five-sixths of a year or ten months. From that time on, having struck his gait, the Tape Reader can, without increasing his unit to over 1200 shares, make $900 a week or $46,- 800 a year.

One trader who for years has been trying to scalp the market and who could never quite overcome the "kitty," reports that his first attempts at applying these rules resulted in a loss of about $20 per trade. This he gradually reduced to $12, then to $8, finally succeeding in throwing the balance over to the credit side and is now able to make a daily profit of from $12 to $30 per 100 shares. This is doing very well indeed. I have no doubt that his profits will continue to increase.

Some people seem to hold the opinion that as the profits desired are only ⅛ average per trade one should limit himself in taking profits. Perhaps I have not made myself clear in this respect.

I buy and sell when I get my indications. In going into a trade I do not know whether it will show a profit or a loss, or how much. I try to trade at a point where I can secure protection with a stop from ¼ to ½ point away, so that my risk is limited to this fraction plus commission and tax. If the trade goes in my favor I push the stop up as soon as possible, to a point where there can be no loss.

Taking Profits

I do not let profits run blindly but only so long as there appears no indication on which to close. No matter where my stop order stands, I am always on the watch for danger signals. Sometimes I get them way in advance of the time a trade should be closed; in other instances my "get out" will flash onto the tape as suddenly and as clearly defined as a streak of lightning against a black sky.

When the tape says "get out" I never stop to reckon how much profit or loss I have or whether I am ahead or behind on the day. I strive for an increasing average profit but I do not keep my eye so much on the fractions or points made or lost, so much as on myself.

I endeavor to perfect myself in clearheadedness, quickness of thought, accuracy of judgment, promptness in planning and executing my plays, foresight, intuition, courage and initiative. Masterful control of myself in these respects will produce a winning average – it is merely a question of practice.

To show how accurately the method works out in practice, I will describe one recent day's trading in which there were three transactions, involving six orders (three buying and three selling). *The market did not go one-eighth against me in five orders out of the six.* In the sixth, the stock went 5/8 above the selling price at which my order was given. I have never seen nor heard of this feat being accomplished before by anyone in Wall Street. Details follow:

I had no open trades. Kansas City Southern, which had been intensely dull, came on the tape 2600 at 46¾. I gave a buying order and before it could reach the "post" the Tape said 46%. and 47. The stock rose steadily and after selling at 48⅝ and coming back to 48½ I gave the selling order. It has not touched 48⅝ again up to now.

Successful Trades

The next trade was in Reading. I saw that it was being held in check in spite of its great strength. The stock had opened at 158. After a certain bulge I saw the reaction coming. When it arrived, and the stock was selling at 157½, I gave the buying order, got mine at 157⅝ and it has not been there since. It immediately rose to 158¾. I noted selling indications and gave the order while the stock was at that price on the tape. It did not react sufficiently to warrant my picking it up again and later went to 159⅜, which was above my selling indication.

Southern Pacific suddenly loomed up as a winner and I bought it at 135. It promptly went to 135½. The rest of the market began to look temporarily overbulled, so I gave my order to sell when the stock was 135%, which proved to be the highest for the day, making the fifth time out of six orders when my stock moved almost instantly in my favor.

This illustration is not prompted by egotism. It is given as an example of the high percentage of accuracy possible under this method of trading. I do not pretend to be able to accomplish these results except occasionally, but I am constantly striving toward being able to do so in a large percentage of my trades.

If one makes 2⅜ points one day and loses 2 points in the next two days, he is ⅜ ahead for the three days, or an average of ⅛ per day. He may have losing and winning streaks, get discouraged and lose his nerve at times, but if he is made of the right stuff he will in time overcome all obstacles and land at the desired goal.

XII. CLOSING THE TRADES – SUGGESTIONS FOR STUDENTS

THE student of Tape Reading, especially he who puts his knowledge into actual practice, is constantly evolving new ideas and making discoveries which modify or nullify his former methods. From each new elevation he enjoys a broader view; what were obstacles disappear; his problems gradually simplify.

Losses in Closing

We have previously defined Tape Reading as the art of determining the *immediate* trend of prices. If one can do this successfully in the majority of his trades, his profits should roll up. But scenting the trend and getting in right is only one-half of the business. Knowing when to close a trade is just as important, if not the most important part of a complete transaction.

At a certain point in my trading, I. became aware that a large percentage of my losing trades resulted from failure to close at the culmination of what I have termed the immediate trend. An example will make this clear: New York Central was on a certain day the strongest stock in a bull market which showed a tendency to react. The pressure was on Reading and Steel. My indications were all bullish, so I couldn't consistently sell either of the latter short I was looking for an opportunity to buy. The market began to slide off, Reading and Steel being the principal clubs with which the pounding was done. I watched them closely and the moment I saw that the selling of these two stocks had ceased, gave my order to buy New York Central, getting it at 137¼. It never touched there again, and in ten minutes was 139 bid for 5,000 shares. Here I should have sold, as my buying indication was for that particular advance. Especially should I have sold when I saw the rise culminate in a spectacular bid which looked like bait for outside buyers. Of course the stock might have gone higher.

The main trend for the day was upward. But for the time being 139 was the high point. I knew the stock was due to react from this figure, and it did, but at the bottom of the normal reaction selling broke out in fresh quarters and the whole market came down heavily. The result was that my profit was only a fraction of what it ought to have been.

An Error

This is the way the trade might have been made: I should have sold when 139 was noisily bid, and when the reaction had run its course, picked it up again, provided indications were still bullish. If they were not I would have been in the position of looking to get short instead of waiting for a chance to get out of my long.

Taking Quick Profits

Having reserved in the early, part of this series the right to revise my views, I will here record the claim that the best results in Tape Reading lie in scenting the moves which are likely to occur in, say, the next half hour, getting in when they start and out when they culminate. This will in most cases cause failure to get *all* of the moves in the one most active stock for the day, but should result in many small profits, and I believe the final results will exceed those realized by sitting on one stock through reactions.

Changes in Leadership

Objections to the latter method are many. One is, the change in leadership which frequently occurs several times during the same session. It being the purpose of the Tape Reader to keep in the leading stock, he must aim to shift from one issue to another as they come to the front.

It is exasperating to see your stock lose its prominence and "turn dead" on your hands, especially if it occurs at a point where part of the profit has disappeared. And there is little comfort in a half-point profit when some other issue would have shown three times as much. Each day's session should be made to yield the highest possible amount of revenue, just as though it were the last day on which trading could be done, and there seems no better way of obtaining these results than by the latest and most approved method mentioned above.

Keeping the Decks Clear

The decks are thus kept clear for whatever offers; there is no dead wood about.

There is a very wide difference in mental attitude between the man who feels compelled to get out of something and one who is long of money and looking for a chance to make a fresh trade.

The start and finish of one of these small swings is best illustrated by a triangle, the narrow end representing the commencement, and the wide end the culmination. An upward move would appear thus:

and a downward move thus:

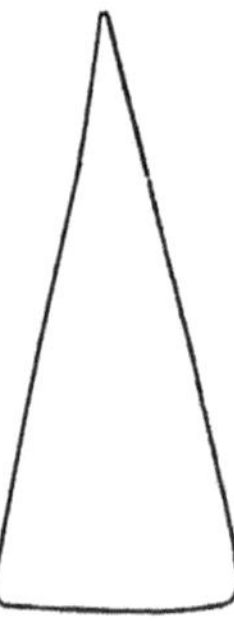

These figures denote the widening character of a move as it progresses and are intended to show how volume, activity and number of transactions expand until, at the end, comparatively riotous conditions prevail. The principle works. the same in the larger swings; witness the spectacular rise in Union Pacific within a few sessions marking the end of the August, 1909, boom.

Getting Ready

After closing out a trade the tape will tell on the following reaction whether you are justified in taking the same stock on again or whether some other issue will pay better. Frequently a stock will be seen preparing for a move two or three swings ahead of the one in which it becomes the leader. This is a fine point, but with study and practice the most complicated indications clarify.

And now a word about the many who are endeavoring to turn this series to practical account. The results which are attainable depend solely upon the individual. Each must work out his own method of trading, based on suggestions derived from these Studies or from other sources. It will doubtless be found that what is one man's meat is another's poison, and that no amount of "book lamin' " will avail if the student does not put his knowledge to an actual test in the market.

Necessity of Study

It is surprising how an acquaintance with subjects relative to the stock market, but seemingly having no bearing upon Tape Reading, will lead to opportunities or aid in making deductions. It is therefore best to study everything possible about the subject And so when asked what books will best supplement these Studies, I should say: Read everything you can get hold of. If you find but a single idea in a publication it is well worth the time and money spent in procuring and studying it.

Wall Street is crowded with men who are there in the hope of making money, but who cannot be persuaded to look at the proposition from a practical business standpoint. Least of all will they study it, for this means long hours of hard work, and Mr. Speculator is laziness personified. Frequently

I have met those who pin their faith to some one point, such as the volumes up or down, and call it Tape Reading. Others, unconsciously trading on mechanical indications, pretend to be reading the tape. Then there is a class of people who read the tape with their tongues, calling off each transaction, a certain accent on the higher or lower quotations indicating whether they are bullish or bearish. These and others in their class are merely operating on the superficial. If they would spend the same five or six hours a day (which they now practically waste) in close study of the *business* of speculation, the result in dollars would be more gratifying at the end of the year. As it is, the majority of them are now losing money.

Scientific Speculation

It is a source of satisfaction, however, that these Studies which, I believe, are the first practical articles ever written on the subject of Tape Reading, have stirred the minds of many people to the possibilities in the line of scientific speculation. Evidence of this is found in the numerous communications received in response to my recent invitation ; many of them from traders situated in remote localities.

In the main, the writers, who are now carrying on long distance operations for the big swings are desirous of testing their ability as Tape Readers. No doubt those who have written represent but a small percentage of the number who are thus inclined.

To all such persons I would . say: Before you can make a success of Tape Reading you must acquire a broad fundamental knowledge of the market. A professional singer who was recently called upon to advise a young aspirant said: "One must become a 'personality' - that is, an intelligence developed by the study of many things besides music." It is not enough to know a few of the underlying principles; one must have a *deep* understanding.

Endless Possibilities

To be sure it is possible for a person to take a number of the "tricks of the trade" herein mentioned and trade successfully on these alone. Even one idea which forms part of the whole subject may be worked and elaborated upon until it becomes a method in itself. There are endless possibilities in this direction., and after all it matters little *how* the money is extracted from the market, so long as it is done legitimately.

But real Tape Reading takes everything into account - every little character which appears on the tape plays its part in forming one of the endless series of "moving pictures." In many years' study of the tape, I do not remember having seen two of these "pictures" which were duplicates. One can realize from this how impossible it would be to formulate a simple set of rules to fit every case or even the majority of them, as each day's session produces hundreds of situations, which, so far as memory serves, are never repeated.

The subject of Tape Reading is therefore practically inexhaustible, which makes it all. the more interesting to the man who has acquired the "study habit."

Practical Study

Having fortified himself with the necessary fundamental knowledge, the student of Tape Reading should thoroughly digest these Studies and any others which may be obtainable in future. It is not enough to go over and over a lesson as a school boy does, driving the facts into his head by monotonous repetition; tapes must be procured and the various indications matched up with what has been studied. And even after one believes he understands, he will presently learn that, to quote the words of a certain song, "You don't know how much you know until you know how little you know." One of my teachers in another line of study used to make me go over a thing three or four times after I *thought* I knew it, just to make sure that I did.

I should say that it is almost impossible for one who has never before traded from the tape to go into a broker's office, start right in and operate successfully. In the first place, there are the abbreviations and all the little characters and their meanings to be learned. It is not enough to know the abbreviations of the principal stocks; it is necessary to know *everything* that appears on the tape, so that nothing will be overlooked. Otherwise the operator will be like a person who attempts to read classic literature without knowing words of more than four letters.

Floor Trading

It is a common impression in the Street that anyone who has the price can buy a seat on the Stock Exchange and at once begin making money as a floor trader. But as has already been shown in THE TICKER, floor trading is a business that one has to learn, and it usually takes months and years to become accustomed to the physical and nervous strain and learn the ropes.

Frequent requests are made for the name of someone who will teach the Art of Tape Reading. I do not know of anyone able to read the tape with profit who is willing to become an instructor. The reason is very simple. Profits from the tape far exceed anything that might be earned in tuition fees.

In addition to the large operators and floor traders who use Tape Reading in their daily work, there are a number of New York Stock Exchange members who never go on the floor, but spend the session at the ticker in their respective offices. Experience has taught them that they can produce larger profits by this method, else they would not follow it. The majority of them trade in 500-share lots and. up and their business forms an inportant share of the daily volume.

Intuitive Tape Reading

A number of so-called semi-professionals operate on what may be termed intuitive tape reading. They have no well defined code of rules and probably could not explain clearly just how they do it, but they "get the money" and that is the best proof of the pudding.

The existence of even a comparatively small body of successful Tape Readers is evidence that money making by this means is an accomplished fact and should encourage others.

One of the greatest difficulties which the novice has to overcome is known by the slangy but expressive term, "cold feet." Too many people start and dabble a little without going far enough to determine whether or not they can make a go of it. And even those who get pretty well along in the subject will be scared to death at a string of losses and quit just when they should dig in harder.

For in addition to learning the art they must form a sort of trading character, which no amount of reverses can discourage nor turn back and which constantly strives to eliminate its own weak points such as fear, greed, anxiety, nervousness and the many other mental factors which go to make or unmake the profit column.

A Trading Character

Perhaps I have painted a difficult proposition. If so, the greater will be the reward of those who master it. As stated at the beginning, Tape Reading is hard work. There seems no good reason for altering that opinion.

If these Studies and those in the series which will follow are the means of adding a few more names to the list of successful speculators, whether they are Tape Readers or not, I shall feel compensated.

THE END

www.ingramcontent.com/pod-product-compliance
Lightning Source LLC
Chambersburg PA
CBHW060546200326
41521CB00007B/503

* 9 7 8 1 6 6 7 3 0 6 4 1 4 *